The Holy Spirit Within Us

The Holy Spirit Within Us

By Bill C. Konstantopoulos

Warner Press®
Anderson, Indiana

Coordinator of Publishing & Creative Services
Church of God Ministries, Inc.
PO Box 2420
Anderson, IN 46018-2420
800-848-2464
www.chog.org

To purchase additional copies of this book, to inquire about distribution, and for all other sales-related matters, please contact:

Warner Press, Inc.
PO Box 2499
Anderson, IN 46018-2499
800-741-7721
www.warnerpress.org

Cover and layout design by Curtis D. Corzine
Edited by Joseph D. Allison and Stephen R. Lewis.

ISBN-13: 978-1-59317-512-2

Printed in the United States of America.

POD: LSI

In humble gratitude

to my wife,

Kay Konstantopoulos,

and

to my spiritual mentor,

Menelaus Katsarkas

Table of Contents

Preface

Truth is the most liberating force in the world. Our Lord confirmed this when he said, "You will know the truth, and the truth will make you free" (John 8:32).

Our culture today is more geared toward that which is instant, gratifying, and convenient. We place a priority on whatever advances our ambition and meets our craving for pleasure, instead of what is right, just, and truthful. So we are reluctant to seek the truth and embrace it. In the words of the scripture, we are "exchanging the truth for a lie." Because we have lost both the discipline and the desire for truth, we shy away from anything that calls for *surrender, sacrifice,* and *abandonment.* These words have almost vanished from the Christian vocabulary. We have replaced biblical self-denial with the desire for self-realization and fulfillment.

Earnest servants of God are both lovers and students of the truth. As John the evangelist says, "I rejoiced greatly when brethren came and testified of the truth that is in you, just as you walk in the truth. I have no greater joy than to hear that my children walk in truth" (3 John 3-4). Every believer needs to rediscover the fundamental truths of the Bible, which provide a solid foundation for spiritual growth and victorious living. The marketplace is filled with glittering substitutes, but we must seek the truth even when it makes us uncomfortable, convicts our souls, and—through the power of the Holy Spirit—transforms our lives.

In the following pages you will come face-to-face with some of these biblical truths which are transformational in nature. They are not treated in an exhaustive way, but simply, in order to entice you to explore and experience them.

Some time ago I was invited to share at the Inter-American Conference of the Church of God in Santiago, Chile; at the Church of God in Caguas, Puerto Rico; and at the Virginia state camp meeting. At each of these, I was asked to address some of the biblical truths that appear to be neglected in our generation. At the Santiago Conference, I dealt with "Sanctification and the Life of Holiness" and "The Gift of the Holy Spirit and the Gift of Tongues"; in Puerto Rico, "The Steps of Sanctification"; and in Virginia, "The Quest for Holiness." This book grew out of the materials shared in these conferences.

It was my aim to be practical and brief, above all remaining true to the biblical text as God enabled me to see and state it. Certainly, my approach will not satisfy everyone and will not answer all questions, but if it creates a desire to know more about the work of the Holy Spirit, as well as bring some conviction and commitment to seek the truth further, my goal will have been achieved. I will leave the outcome to the Holy Spirit himself. After all, He is the teacher of truth.

We may disagree when it comes to our approaches and definitions, but as earnest believers we should be willing to accept and abide by the irrefutable truth which is stated in the Word of God. Truth never needs artful interpretation, simply belief and obedience.

I hope and pray that this book will ignite a flame in your soul to seek and experience a life of holiness, because God has predestined you to be conformed to the image of His Son, Jesus Christ.

Bill C. Konstantopoulos

Acknowledgments

L ife has dreams and aspirations, plans and goals. Some want to climb Everest; others delight to explore the oceans. Some yearn to engrave their names in places which defy decay, while others humbly serve and make a difference in the lives of people, even if they are never recognized.

My observation is that we owe everything to the grace of God. I cannot imagine any way that I could be where I am today without the grace of God. Being born in an obscure place, untouched by civilization, I had the windows of opportunity opened to me by a visitation of God's grace. God saved me in the person of Jesus Christ, and I count it as life's greatest privilege to know and serve Him, and to be involved in the advancement of His kingdom. All my gratitude and thanks ultimately go to Him.

But life is not an island. God uses other human beings to equip us, encourage us, guide us, and help us for everything that we achieve in life. So it is with this volume that you hold in your hands; it could not have been possible without the help of others.

I have been helped and encouraged by many, but none had as much impact in shaping my life and ministry in so many ways as my wife of forty-three years, Kay. Not only has she helped me to see the funny side of life, but her unmovable faith has encouraged me to attempt things that otherwise I would have probably never attempted. Her commitment to truth and stewardship, her genuine spirit of service, never seeking the spotlight, but always working in the background, and her common sense and wisdom have contributed to all that I have endeavored to do.

I recall with deep emotion in our first pastorate during the 1960s. We had just returned home from Sunday morning service, I guess she sensed my discouragement and without saying a word, she threw both arms around my neck and began to sing: "Do you have any rivers that seem impossible to cross and any mountains that you cannot tunnel through, God specializes in things that are impossible, what He has done for others He will also do for you." Throughout the journey of faith, no matter what the situation, the circumstances, the need, or the obstacle, her words always were, "God will take care of you."

She never hesitated to leave family, sacrifice convenience, and follow me around the world, wherever God led. Her quiet, sweet spirit and love for the people always helped her to forget self and give priority to the kingdom. Her commitment to truth, her faithfulness to the Lord and His church, her sacrificial spirit of service, and her unconditional support stand as pillars in the ministry and have served as a sustaining force. Every time she heard me preach on the Holy Spirit, she would always respond, "You need to write a book on the Holy Spirit." Even though there is very little, if any, in this book of that which she heard me preach, nevertheless, she got her wish.

In my teenage years, God placed on my path a seasoned servant of Christ who was full of the Spirit of Christ, full of the grace of God, full of love and whose sensitivity to the Holy Spirit led him to become my mentor in spiritual matters. He was a man of wisdom and integrity, deeply entrenched into the Word of God. He believed in the fullness of the Spirit as a second crisis experience in the life of the believer. He radiated the Spirit of Christ in all facets of life and he practiced holiness of life.

It was this man, Menelaus Katsarkas, who more than anyone else introduced me to the person and the work of the Holy Spirit. He ignited within my soul an unquenchable desire for the experience of holiness. I was seventeen at the time, so I lacked both knowledge and maturity; but my encounter with the Holy Spirit left no doubt of His presence, power, purity and peace in my life. It was a turning point in my walk with the Lord.

Brother Katsarkas and I parted when I was twenty-four. After that, I saw him probably two or three times, but the impact of his life on mine has never been erased. Even though he experienced a lot of difficulties in the later years of his life (the loss of sight, amputations, etc.), yet he maintained his spiritual radiance and walked in the spirit of holiness with such an integrity that he continued to inspire others and glorify the Lord Jesus Christ. I thank God for this man and for his influence on my life. He exemplified what you will read about here.

I owe a great deal to my former church secretary, Ruth Ann Sartain, who has typed this manuscript. She is the only one who can read my handwriting and understand the workings of my mind.

Also, I would like to express my deep gratitude and thanks to Joseph Allison whose expertise, counsel, wisdom, suggestions, and recommendations, combined with the spirit of a Christian gentleman, proved to be invaluable. Without his help and that of his team and Warner Press, this volume would not have been possible. The credit belongs to them.

I.

Fundamental Truths
about the
HOLY SPIRIT

———————

1. *"The Promise of My Father"*

The role of the Holy Spirit in the life of God's people is a theme that appears like a golden thread interwoven throughout the message of the Bible. The Holy Spirit is a person, the third person of the Holy Trinity. He administers the grace of God and equips God's people to fulfill God's call. He appears in all that God does in biblical times, from Creation to the Incarnation; from anointing the prophets to the helping of the children of God through intercession in prayer; from transforming Saul to another man to baptizing the disciples on the day of Pentecost. He is manifested as the power, wisdom and holiness of God, as the energizer of both the church and the kingdom of God. Rightly the Lord says through His prophet that people serve him "'not by might nor by power, but by My Spirit,' says the LORD of hosts" (Zech 4:6).

It is therefore ironic that one of the great controversies among the people of God is over the Holy Spirit and His role in the life of the believer. Many things attributed to Him are not His by nature, because His overarching purpose is to unify the body of Christ. You see, the Holy Spirit is more than a doctrine that should be studied and analyzed. He is a person who must be experienced and through whom we must be related to one another in divine love, *koinonia*.

The Holy Spirit is promised as God's gift to every believer. "Peter said to them, 'Repent, and each of you be baptized in the name of Jesus Christ for the forgiveness of your sins; and you will receive the gift of the Holy Spirit'" (Acts 2:38). Jesus said to His disciples, "And behold, I am sending forth the promise of My Father upon you; but you are to stay in the city until you are clothed with power from on high" (Luke 24:49). This promise is clarified in the Gospel of John: "I will ask the Father, and He will give you another Helper, that He may be with you forever; that is the Spirit of truth, whom the world cannot receive, because it does not see Him or know Him, but you know Him because He abides with you and will be in you" (John 14:16–17; in the Greek, "another helper" is *allon paraklhton*—one who bends at your side in time of need in order to help).

We must look into the Old Testament to learn more about this promise of the Father. There the prophet Joel says: "It will come about after this that I will pour out My Spirit on all mankind; and your sons and daughters will prophesy, your old men will dream dreams, your young men will see visions. Even on the male and female servants I will pour out My Spirit in those days" (Joel 2:28-29). The apostle Peter says that this was fulfilled on the day of Pentecost ("but this is what was spoken of through the prophet Joel," Acts 2:16), and then he says, "For the promise is for you and your children and for all who are far off, as many as the Lord our God will call to Himself" (Acts 2:39). In that day, the Holy Spirit came upon God's people with great power.

The Lord Jesus Christ further expounded and clarified the work of the Holy Spirit. He told the disciples "to wait for what the Father had promised, 'Which...you heard of from Me; for John baptized with water, but you will be baptized with the Holy Spirit not many days from now'" (Acts 1:4–5). "The Helper, the Holy Spirit, whom the Father will send in My name, He will teach you all things, and bring to your remembrance all that I said to you" (John 14:26).

Notice that the promise of the Father, the promise of the Son, the promise of the apostles, and the testimony of the early church all agree upon this point: The Holy Spirit will come upon believers. Our Lord identifies the Holy Spirit as our helper, guide, and teacher. He will empower us and set us on the path of growth and spiritual maturity. To that end, that we are admonished to "be filled with the Spirit" (Eph 5:18); "walk by the Spirit" (Gal 5:16, 25); "live by the Spirit" (Gal 6:25); and be "led by the Spirit" (Gal 5:18), "for the law of the Spirit of life in Christ Jesus has set you free from the law of sin and death" (Rom 8:2).

The promise of the gift of the Holy Spirit upon our lives (or, if you prefer, "the infilling of the Holy Spirit" or "the fullness of the Spirit") encompasses several aspects of our relationship with Him:

A. His presence with us and in us.
B. His power upon us.
C. His purity within us and His sanctification of us.
D. His perpetuation in us by His fruit.
E. His preparation of us by equipping us through the gifts for edification.
F. The promise of the gift, its perception, the biblical principles and the practice of the gift of tongues.

The Promise of His Presence
On the day of Pentecost, the Holy Spirit came upon the disciples in the Upper Room. It was not an illusion. The Comforter had come to be with them and in them. From that day forward, every believer can experience the indwelling presence of the Holy Spirit. It is to that end that the scripture says, we "have been made partakers of the Holy Spirit" (Heb 6:4). The fact that tongues of fire appeared on each one of them signified the literal presence of the supernatural Spirit. It is impossible to experience the presence of the Holy Spirit and not know it.

11

Because the disciples were conscious of the presence of the Holy Spirit, they could say, "For it seemed good to the Holy Spirit" (Acts 15:28). The Holy Spirit told Peter, "Behold, three men are looking for you" (10:19). The Holy Spirit told Phillip, "Go up and join this chariot" (8:29). In one case, the Holy Spirit hindered Paul and his companions from going to Bithynia (16:7).

It is the presence of the Holy Spirit within us that makes us "a dwelling of God in the Spirit" (Eph 2:22) and "a temple of the Holy Spirit" (1 Cor 6:19). The Holy Spirit teaches us all things about the kingdom of God (John 14:26), guides us into all truth (16:13), reminds us of the words of Christ (14:26), and convicts the world of sin, righteousness, and judgment (16:8). The presence of the Holy Spirit

- *conditions* us to be spiritually minded,
- *convinces* us of the truth of God's word,
- *convicts* us of sin and wrong,
- *compels* us to a life of holiness,
- *consumes* us with the passion of Christ,
- *conforms* us to the image of Christ, and
- *controls* both our attitude and outlook in life.

It is His presence that changes us to become like Christ himself. We "being transformed into the same image from glory to glory, just as from *the Lord, the Spirit*" (2 Cor 3:18, italics added). So the Holy Spirit has become an indwelling presence in our lives.

The Promise of His Power

The Lord Jesus Christ said that the Holy Spirit would bring his disciples spiritual power. "You will receive power when the Holy Spirit has come upon you" (Acts 1:8). "You are to stay in the city until you are clothed with power from on high" (Luke 24:49). Wherever the Spirit is present and at work, there is power. We can neither be spiritual nor do spiritual things without the power of the Holy Spirit. Even the Lord Jesus went forth "in the power of the Spirit" (Luke 4:14).

Notice the manifestations of power at the coming of the Holy Spirit. On the day of Pentecost, He came in the upper room as a "rushing mighty wind" (Acts 2:2, KJV), a powerful force that liberated the disciples from fear and made them bold for witness. The same is evident in the fourth chapter of Acts, which says that when the disciples prayed and were all filled with the Spirit, their meeting place was shaken and they boldly testified of Christ. We are powerless to confront the Enemy and become passionate witnesses to the love of Christ without the power of the Holy Spirit.

Only the Holy Spirit's power can enable us to serve effectively, minister effectively, witness authentically and preach persuasively.

The Promise of His Purity
After the outpouring of the Holy Spirit upon the household of Cornelius, the apostle Peter reported to the Council in Jerusalem that God, who knows the heart, testified to them giving them the Holy Spirit, just as He also did to us; and He made no distinction between us and them, *cleansing their hearts by faith*" (Acts 15:8–9, italics added). This underscores the fact that it is the work of the Holy Spirit to purify, sanctify and make us holy. Thus, John the Baptist said, "He will baptize you with the Holy Spirit and fire" (Matt 3:11; Luke 3:16). Fire represents the cleansing power of the Holy Spirit.

The coming of the Holy Spirit will purge us from spiritual deadness. He purifies our thoughts, our feelings, our will, and our motives, and sets our feet on the highway of holiness.

The Promise of Spiritual Fruit
In his letter to the Galatians, the apostle Paul outlines the fruit of the Spirit in the life of the Christian as being "love, joy,

peace, patience, kindness, goodness, faithfulness, gentleness, self-control" (Gal 5:22–23). We will discuss these in detail in Chapter 3.

For now, let us note that the fruit of the Spirit bring freedom, health, and prosperity to the soul. In essence, the fruit is what the Spirit does in us in order to enhance our life and our relationship with the Father. The fruit is the ministry of the Holy Spirit within us.

Everyone who is filled with the Holy Spirit bears the fruit of the Spirit but not necessarily the gifts of the Spirit. Gifts of the Spirit cannot function in the life of the believer without the fruit of the Spirit.

God promises to place us in His Kingdom and give us everything necessary to do the life mission that He has for us. Our only responsibility concerning a spiritual gift is that we use it properly to its fullest extent for the purpose that God intended it to be used. However, all of us as believers are expected to surrender to the Holy Spirit and allow Him to fill us with His fruit. Though we cannot choose what gifts God's Spirit may give us, we can choose whether to allow the fruit of the Spirit to be manifested in our lives. There is no reason why a believer who has yielded to the Spirit should not be rich in spiritual fruit.

The Promise of Anointing

The early church held many councils in an effort to understand the identity and nature of the Holy Spirit. Ironically, most controversies about the Holy Spirit in our day are not about his identity, but His manifestations. It seems that many more people want to experience the Spirit's manifestations than the Spirit himself.

One controversy is over the anointing of the Spirit. The Greek word *chrisma* comes from the word *chrio* (to anoint, especially to anoint with oil), which appears several times in the Septuagint Greek version of the Old Testament (e.g., Ex

29:7; 30:25). However, the word is used only four times in the New Testament (1 John 2:20, 27) and is combined with the words *echete* (you possess), *elabete* (you received), *menei* (abides in you), or *didaskei* (teaches you). These passages seem to emphasize that the Spirit's anointing was something that the readers had already experienced as confirmation of their calling and work (see 1 Pet 2:5, 9). The anointing of God is indispensable in our lives.

The anointing of the Spirit signifies a calling to be separated for God to an office of service or ministry. Simply, it is a call to serve God. Thus, the Spirit of God came upon Samson and John the Baptist. Similarly, the Spirit of God came upon Paul, identifying him as God's apostle to the Gentiles.

The Spirit's anointing equips us to speak boldly, unfolding the Word of God with revelation, clarity and authority. Jesus says, "The spirit of the Lord is upon me, because he anointed me to preach the gospel to the poor. He has sent me to proclaim release to the captives" (Luke 4:18–19, quoting from Is 61:1).

Today, many people suppose that they can manipulate the Spirit's anointing or even impart it to others. Not true. You can be faithful, obedient, and totally submissive to the Lord, but you do not have control over the anointing of the Spirit. It is like the wind. It comes at God's choosing. It will not make you get out of the order of God. It is not intended to make you feel super spiritual. The anointing of the Spirit comes to fulfill the purpose of God and that is all. It is not for the purpose of self-gratification.

The Promise of Gifts for Service

A second area of modern controversy concerns the *charismata* or "gifts" of the Holy Spirit. The singular is *charisma*, which derives from the Greek word *charizomai* (to show grace). It is a gift of grace or undeserved benefit. In the New Testament, it is only used for gifts and graces imparted by God (see 1 Cor 7:7). A *charisma* is the Holy Spirit's instantaneous enablement of

15

any believer to exercise a gift for the edification of others or the church. The Bible speaks freely of the gifts of the Spirit, and it is evident that when these are in operation, the church is both edified and perfected, and disciples are equipped for ministry.

The apostle Paul lists the primary gifts of the Spirit in Ephesians 4:11-13: "And He gave some as apostles, and some as prophets, and some as evangelists, and some as pastors and teachers." The primary purpose of these gifts is to equip Christ's followers to do the work of the ministry. A secondary purpose is to edify the body of Christ and assist each other in the work of the ministry, for the glorification of Jesus Christ.

The apostle Paul says in 1 Corinthians 12:7, "But to each one is given the manifestation [singular, *phanerosis*] of the Spirit for the common good." Then he begins to name those gifts: wisdom, knowledge, faith, healing, working of miracles, prophecy, discerning of spirits, and different kinds of tongues. All of these are aids to ministry. Their purpose is to edify the church, to improve and direct its life; and all of these gifts work in harmony.

When the Holy Spirit is in control of our lives, not only will the church be seasoned with the spirit of holiness and unity, but everything will be done in order, and our corporate life will bring glory to God. Let's allow the Holy Spirit to administer the church and build the kingdom of God by distributing the gifts as it pleases Him. Then and only then will we properly function in the church. Then and only then will the church advance according to the plan of God.

2. Sanctification and the Life of Holiness

We cannot ignore or lightly regard three passages of Scripture which call us to a life of holiness. The first is Paul's declaration to the Christians in Thessaloniki, "For this is the will of God, your sanctification: that you should abstain from sexual immorality…For God did not call us to uncleanness, but in holiness" (1 Thess 4:3, 7 NKJV). Paul then prays that they might experience this: "Now may the God of peace Himself sanctify you entirely; and may your spirit and soul and body be preserved complete, without blame at the coming of our Lord Jesus Christ. Faithful is He who calls you, and He also will bring it to pass" (1 Thess 5:23–24).

The second scripture is the admonition of the writer of Hebrews to the people of God as far as their conduct in the world is concerned and their relationship with other human beings, especially those of the household of faith, "Pursue peace with all people, and holiness, without which no one will see the Lord" (Heb 12:14 NKJV). The same writer informs us that God chastens us so "that we might be partakers of His holiness" (Heb 12:10 NKJV).

Third, the apostle Paul informs us that God has predestined us—not, as some think, to be lost or to be saved, but rather to a life of godliness. Every believer "He also predestined to become conformed to the image of His Son, so that He would be the firstborn among many brethren" (Rom 8:29).

If we examine these biblical texts in their totality, we will be struck by the fact that sanctification and holiness are central to the Christian experience. The Bible underscores the message that God wills and commands us to be holy. The cry of the heart of the redeemed is for holiness. It is the goal of the Christian life to be conformed to the image of Christ or to achieve Christlikeness.

Sanctification is God's high standard for His people. It is what makes them unique and distinct among all the peoples of the earth. Therefore, Scripture clearly expounds the process of this experience through the working of the Holy Spirit. It is not our intent here to do a complete theological exposition on the subject but to focus on the basic aspects of sanctification as they are related in God's Word and thus allow the Holy Spirit to convict, convince, compel, and counsel us concerning this experience.

Before we do, I feel compelled to say a few words about contemporary attitudes concerning the truth of holiness and sanctification. One of the most disturbing signs of our day is the embarrassing silence of the Christian pulpit when it comes to the message of holiness and the widespread neglect of such an experience. History has taught us that the stance of the pulpit always determines the state of the people. The church loses influence, authority, integrity, and missional effectiveness when the character of holiness is absent and when the church ceases to bear the marks of Christ.

In writing to the Roman Christians, the apostle Paul unfolds this truth by declaring, "But now having been set free from sin, and having become slaves of God, you have your fruit to holiness, and the end, everlasting life" (Rom 6:22 NKJV). "For the law of the Spirit of life in Christ Jesus has made me free from the law of sin and death" (Rom 8:2). To the Corinthians, he writes, "Therefore, if anyone is in Christ, he is a new creature; the old things passed away; behold, new things have come" (2 Cor 5:17).

In the rest of the epistles, we find more illuminating statements from the apostle concerning the life of holiness: "It was for freedom that Christ set us free; therefore keep standing firm and do not be subject again to a yoke of slavery" (Gal 5:1). "Walk by the Spirit, and you will not carry out the desire of the flesh" (Gal 5:16). "For the grace of God has appeared, bringing salvation to all men, instructing us to deny ungodliness and worldly desires and to live sensibly, righteously and godly in the present age" (Titus 2:11–12).

It is evident from such passages that God has a behavioral code for His people, and that is holiness in all levels of our lives. When the grace of God saves us through the blood of Christ and the Holy Spirit lives within us, we become partakers of the divine nature. Both our attitude and outlook are controlled by the Holy Spirit. Both our emotional and mental states begin to reflect the mind of Christ and are seasoned with the fruit of the Spirit.

In the light of such clear New Testament teaching, it will be evident to any believer that the Lord requires sanctification of the heart and holiness of life, and that such an experience comes only by the working power of the Holy Spirit. But believers differ in their definition of those terms, their understanding of when sanctification can occur in the Christian life, and what really is the outcome of this experience. Without endeavoring to split theological hairs, let us consider what is clear and inescapable in the biblical message.

God calls us to a holy life. Our hearts cry out for a divine intervention to grant us spiritual victory and cleansing from inner sin. Indeed, God promises us deliverance and cleansing as we surrender to the infilling of the Holy Spirit.

The holiness that God promises is *relational* in nature. It affects our relationship with God, our relationship with ourselves, our relationship with the body of Christ, as well as our relationship with other human beings. So we may say that the scope of holiness is *inclusive*. It energizes the totality of our being and life.

If we were going to define the two terms, *sanctification* and *holiness*, we could say,

> *Sanctification* is the baptism of the Holy Spirit that cleanses the heart from sin so that His indwelling presence can empower the believer for life and service. Sanctification is deliverance from inner conflict, producing rest in the presence of God. It is full surrender to God and perfection in His love.

> *Holiness* is the outward manifestation of the inward work of Christ in the believer. The essence of holiness is Christlikeness. It is the culture of God's kingdom.

W. Stanley Johnson says that John Wesley defined holiness as "love for God that results in love for others and cleansing of the heart from the old inadequacy of our evil imagination that found rest in a fundamentally idolatrous attitude toward some things or passions, a center of values other than God."[1]

The Bible definitely calls the believer to sanctification of heart and holiness of life. The Greek text employs certain words to enhance our understanding of this experience and guide us into it.

The first word is *hagiazo* (to sanctify, to make holy, to cleanse). This word has a double meaning. First, it can indicate that something or someone has been set apart for a particular use, as in the case of the vessels in the temple, which were exclusively dedicated to be used in the worship of God. Any other use constituted defilement. In this sense, the word is sometimes translated as *consecrate*, as when Jesus said in John 17:19, "I sanctify myself." Second, *hagiazo* can mean "to make

---

1. W. Stanley Johnson, "Christian Perfection as Love for God," *Wesleyan Theological Journal*, Spring 1983, 18:1, 57-58.

holy," "to alter," or "to transform," especially as it refers to a person's behavior. This is why the Bible always addresses its call for sanctification or holiness to the believer. Paul writing to the Roman Christians extends his admonition to them with these words, "I urge you, brethren, by the mercies of God, to present your bodies a living and holy sacrifice, acceptable to God, which is your spiritual service of worship. And do not be conformed to this world, but be transformed by the renewing of your mind, so that you may prove what the will of God is, that which is good and acceptable and perfect" (Rom 12:1–2).

We should briefly mention two other words in the New Testament Greek text. One is *hagiasmos* (sanctification). At times, our English versions translate the word *hagiasmos* as "holiness." Romans 6 has a couple of examples: "so now present your members as slaves to righteousness, resulting in sanctification" (v 19) and "resulting in sanctification" (v 22). The other word is *hagiosune* (holy character or sanctity). This word occurs only three times in the New Testament: Romans 1:4; 2 Corinthians 7:1; and 1 Thessalonians 3:13. In each of these instances, it denotes qualities of character.

All three of these Greek words emphasize that sanctification is the Holy Spirit's work of cleansing and delivering the human heart from the instinct or desire to sin while holiness is an expression of that work in all areas of our life and relationships. This is why the apostle Paul says, "For just as you presented your members as slaves of uncleaness…so now present your members as slaves of righteousness for holiness." (Rom 6:19 NKJV).

Sanctification and holiness are the work of the Holy Spirit in the life of the believer. They are initiated the moment that that the believer surrenders to God and is filled with the Holy Spirit. The Spirit purifies our hearts by faith and sanctifies us wholly, and we are then expected to perfect holiness in the fear of God (2 Cor 7:1).

The work of the Holy Spirit in the believer's heart is definite and complete. He provides freedom and deliverance, holiness and purity, and enables the believer to live victoriously over sin and self. Some say that the old self or Adamic nature is crucified; some say that it is eradicated; others say that it is suppressed. One thing is certain: The believer is set free from the will and desire to sin. Is he capable of sin? Sure! Does he want to sin? No! He has victory over temptation and his love for God insolates him from the love of the world.

This is how the apostle Paul describes such a state to the Romans: "Our old self was crucified with Him...Even so consider yourselves to be dead to sin, but alive to God in Christ Jesus...For sin shall not be master over you...But now having been freed from sin and enslaved to God, you derive your benefit, resulting in sanctification, and the outcome, eternal life" (Rom 6:6, 11, 14, 22). The apostle John states, "No one who is born of God practices sin, because His seed abides in him; and he cannot sin, because he is born of God" (1 John 3:9).

So sanctification delivers us from the carnal nature and puts our human nature in subjection to the will of God. It frees us from the will to sin, although we are still subject to temptation and the possibility of sin. The Holy Spirit not only cleanses us, but empowers us for holy living and service. The believer receives this experience subsequent to conversion by an act of consecration and faith. It is the instantaneous work of the Holy Spirit, although progress and growth continue for a lifetime as we continue to receive grace, knowledge, and wisdom.

There is a danger that we might accept sanctification as a Bible doctrine and fail to have the experience itself. How can we know whether the Holy Spirit has changed us?

We have said that holiness expresses the sanctification of the heart in all levels of our life. It is a life that conforms to the image of Jesus Christ and seeks to be like Him in everything we do. How is this holiness expressed in a practical way in our daily walk of life?

First, *holiness transforms our relationship with God*. The Holy Spirit perfects the fear of God and the love of God in us. We give God priority in our life. We seek His kingdom before anything else. We are eager to do God's will and obey His Word. We love Him supremely with all our heart, mind, strength, and soul. The experience of holiness makes prayer a delightful experience and an intimate encounter. It makes us sensitive to His guidance and submissive to all that His nature requires of us.

Second, *holiness transforms our relationship with ourselves.* All begins with the heart. The state of our heart determines everything else in life. The Bible says, "Watch over your heart with all diligence, for from it flow the springs of life" (Pro 4:23). Jesus says that "the mouth speaks out of that which fills the heart" (Matt 12:34). The Bible tells us, "The heart is more deceitful than all else and is desperately sick; who can understand it?" (Jer 17:9). The person who walks in holiness is full of the love of God and fruit of the Spirit. This person's heart is free from jealousy, envy, bitterness, and resentment. It enjoys the rest and peace of the Lord and it is always moved with love.

Third, *holiness transforms our relationship within the body of Christ, the church*. We have said before that the experience of sanctification frees us from the barriers that cause disunity and conflict. It changes our disposition toward all people, including the people of God The experience of sanctification fills us with love for our brethren in the manner described in the New Testament: "By this all men will know that you are My disciples, if you have love for one another" (John 13:35). "We know that we have passed out of death into life, because we love the brethren. He who does not love abides in death" (1 John 3:14). Holiness baptizes the body of Christ with love.

Most conflicts that we face in the church have nothing to do with disputes about the truth; they are due to a lack of love. Divine love bridges over all personal differences and brings people together. The unity of sanctified believers is manifested in sacrificial love, hospitality and service. In fact, holiness frees us from the bondage of individualism and empowers us with the spirit of acceptance and service that characterize the Spirit of Christ.

Fourth, *holiness transforms our relationships with the world in which we live.* We have been admonished by Scripture not to love the world or the things that are in the world (1 John 2:15). This does not mean that God alienates us from the people of the world, but rather from the spirit by which the world operates. You see, holiness provides a culture within the kingdom of God that is distinctly different from the culture of the world. We are citizens of another country; as such, we should be the light and salt of the world. Sadly, in today's society there appears to be little difference between the children of God and the children of the world. Holiness in conversation and conduct should distinguish the children of God from the world. Holiness separates us from others and imprints upon us the marks of Christ.

Fifth, *holiness transforms our relationship with our own will.* Holiness liberates us from the inner conflict between our will and God's will. It brings an end to our striving for prominence, possessions, and position. It alters our emotional and mental attitude as well as disposition. We are no longer driven by the will of self, but by the will of God. In that sense, we can say with Paul that the body is dead to sin and the spirit alive in Christ. Sin no longer has dominion over us and the world loses its grip on us. Thus, we are the holy temple of God because the Spirit of God abides in us.

In conclusion, we should note that holiness is spiritual power as well as spiritual liberty. Jesus said, "But you will receive power when the Holy Spirit has come upon you" (Acts 1:8). How is that spiritual power expressed in our daily lives?

First, since the Holy Spirit fills us with the love of God, He empowers us to fear God and worship Him with all our heart, soul, mind and strength.

Second, since the Holy Spirit unites us with other Christians everywhere, He gives us the power to transcend differences of creed, race, social status, and ethnicity. Scripture says of the first Christians, "the congregation of those who believed were of one heart and soul" (Acts 4:32). All the tensions within the body of Christ can be healed by the power of the Holy Spirit, because he changes our hearts and alters our behavior.

Third, the Holy Spirit gives us the power to resist temptation. Holiness does not free us from temptation; however, the power of temptation lies in the desires of our heart and the lust of our flesh. When the Holy Spirit transforms us, our temptation no longer comes from within but from without.

Fourth, the Holy Spirit gives us the power to change our disposition and our attitude toward God, other people, and the circumstances of life. He gives us a disposition of kindness, joy, and hope, free from competitiveness and vindictive expressions. The Spirit enables us to follow the scripture that says, "Finally, brethren, whatever is true, whatever is honorable, whatever is right, whatever is pure, whatever is lovely, whatever is of good repute, if there is any excellence and if anything worthy of praise, dwell on these things" (Phil 4:8).

Fifth, the Holy Spirit gives us power for witness and service. Observers can say about us what was said about the New Testament church: "And with great power the apostles were giving testimony to the resurrection of the Lord Jesus, and abundant grace was upon them all" (Acts 4:33). This power enables us to communicate the love of God for the redemption of the world. "Now to Him who is able to do far more abundantly beyond all that we ask or think, *according to the power that works within us*, to Him be the glory in the church and in Christ Jesus to all generations forever and ever" (Eph 3:20–21, italics added).

3. A Closer Look at the Fruit of the Spirit

In our effort to magnify the person and the work of the Holy Spirit in the life of the believer and the church, we Christians have said a great deal about the gifts of the Spirit; but we hear very little about the fruit of the Spirit. The gifts have to do with enablement, and they can be imitated or counterfeited. But the fruit of the Spirit is His very nature, and it cannot be counterfeited.

There are two words in the Greek New Testament which are used extensively to define our spiritual state. One of these words is *sarkikos*, meaning "carnal or of the flesh, pertaining to the dominance of the flesh or the body." The apostle Paul makes reference to the Corinthian Christians as *sarkikoi* or carnal; they were influenced by the flesh or they followed the principles of the flesh. To be carnal minded is death. In fact, in Galatians, he says that "the flesh sets its desire against the Spirit" (5:17). He names all the works of the flesh and then follows with this admonition: "Walk by the Spirit, and you will not carry out the desires of the flesh" (5:16). To be carnal is enmity to God.

The second word is *pneumatikos*, meaning "spiritual." This word describes what is pertaining to or proceeding from the Holy Spirit. It means that the person is both enlightened and influenced by the Holy Spirit. You cannot bear spiritual fruit unless you are spiritual, and you cannot be spiritual unless you *walk* in the Spirit and *live* in the Spirit, being *influenced* and *controlled* by the Spirit.

Our Lord Jesus Christ gave us the promise that He was going to send another *paraclete*, or helper, to be with us, to abide in us, to teach us all things, and to guide us into all truth, and thus be overshadowed by His presence (John 14,-16). Then the apostle Paul teaches us certain things concerning the Holy Spirit so that we should not be ignorant. From Paul's teaching, we conclude that it is impossible to understand the Bible, the structure of the church or Christian living without some understanding of the person and the work of the Holy Spirit.

The Holy Spirit is co-equal with God. He is a person. He is God, and He is eternal. He is referred to in the New Testament a hundred times as the Holy Spirit. He possesses absolute holiness, absolute purity, and absolute righteousness. The Holy Spirit convicts of sin, and the apostle Paul tells us that we are sealed with the Holy Spirit (Eph 1:13).

The Bible speaks a great deal about the fruitfulness of the Christian life. Jesus said, "You will know them by their fruits" (Matt 7:16; also v. 20). Again He says, "he who abides in Me and I in him, he bears much fruit, for apart from Me you can do nothing" (John 15:5). Then the Bible says that the Spirit of God produces His fruit in our life, and the apostle Paul contrasts the fruit of the Spirit with the works of the flesh.

You see, we are either governed by the flesh or by the Spirit. If you are governed by the flesh, you are carnal, you think carnally and you act carnally. If you are governed by the Spirit, you are spiritual, you think spiritually and act spiritually, and you have the fruit of the Spirit. You cannot produce the fruit of the Spirit by discipline or any other way. We need the Holy Spirit in order to have the fruit. It was the Holy Spirit that brought conviction to our heart, the Holy Spirit led us to repentance, and He helped us to accept Christ as our Savior. But we must yield; we must surrender to the Holy Spirit, so that

He can abide in us, if we want the fruit of the Spirit in our life. The manifestation of the fruit of the Spirit is the most practical evidence that our life is under the control of the Holy Spirit. The thoughts of our mind, the feelings of our heart, the disposition of our will, and the actions of our life reveal, in a practical way, who is in charge of our life. "But the fruit of the Spirit is, " says Paul, and he names nine: "love, joy, peace, patience, kindness, goodness, faithfulness, gentleness, self-control" (Gal 5:22–23). Some of the translations may exchange some of the words, but the number remains the same. The nature of the fruit of the Spirit is divided in three categories: relational, restorative, and protective.

First, the fruit of the Spirit that is relational. The fruit of the Spirit, says Paul, are love (*agape*), patience (*makrothumia*), and gentleness (*praotes*). These help us maintain the right relationship with the Lord, the people of God, and the world. The fruit of the Spirit is love. If you love, that takes care of all the rest. Henry Ward Beecher said, "The mother of all things in the soul is love." Rightly Paul says, "The greatest of these is love" (1 Cor 13:13). And the beloved disciple John affirms it with these words, "We know that we have passed out of death into life, because we love the brethren" (1 John 3:14). This love is both vertical and horizontal. We love God, and we love His people. In the Greek language in which most of the New Testament was written, there are four words for love. The first word is *eros*. It is derived from the name of the son of the goddess Aphrodite, who according to mythology excites erotic love in the gods and men with his arrows and torches. Eros love refers to sensual love. It has to do with sexual love or desire. The second word is *phileo* or *philia*; it is the love between friends or between husband and wife. The third word is *storgé*. This is the love that a mother has for her children. From it we get the Greek word *storgicos*, which means to be extremely moved by love and compassion to the extent that you forget yourself. Thus the scripture says," Can a mother forget her suckling?"

The fourth word is *agape*. This is God's love for us and is the fruit of the Spirit that is in us. This is the love that is shed abroad in our hearts by the Holy Spirit. This is unselfish love. We are incapable of having this love unless we have come to Christ or the Spirit of God abides in us. It is this love that enables us to love God with all our heart, mind, and soul, and our neighbor as ourselves. It is this love that enables us to be of one mind and to have compassion for one another in the body of Christ, the church. It is with this love that we love the people of God, and we are full of both pity and courtesy in our interactions with them. It is this love with which we love the world and the souls of men. Love, such as Christ had, knows no race or face. Real love, which is the fruit of the Spirit, is the love that Christ showed toward mankind. It is this kind of love for God, for the brethren and for the hurting world that will help people know that we are disciples of Christ.

The fruit of the Spirit is longsuffering, *makrothumia*. This word means self-restraint before proceeding to action. It is the quality of a person who is able to avenge himself yet refrains from doing so. In essence, it means to be patient when it comes to people or with people and to endure, putting up with things and circumstances. Someone said that longsuffering is letting a man abuse you or cheat you and then forgetting that he has done so. This is why I say that longsuffering is a relational fruit, because you are patient with people and you are putting up with a lot of things in order to maintain the relationship.

The fruit of the Spirit is gentleness, *praotes*. The King James Version translates this as *meekness*. Someone said, "Gentleness is strength that comes to the aid of a need in the spirit of love." Gentleness is an inwrought grace of the soul, and the expression is primarily to God. "It is the attitude of spirit with which we accept God's dealings with us as good, and we do not dispute or resist." Aristotle says *praotes*, or gentleness, is the middle position, standing between two extremes: getting angry without reason and not getting angry at all. Gentleness is getting angry at the right time, in the right measure, and for the right reason.

The word *meekness*, which the King James Version uses, does injustice to the word *praotes*, because *meekness* expresses weakness, and the Greek word does not imply that at all. *Praotes* is a condition of the mind and heart that demonstrates gentleness, not in weakness but in power. It is a balance born in strength of character.

These three fruit of the Spirit—love, longsuffering, and gentleness—put into perspective our relationship with God, the people of God, and the world. Their absence will make a wreck out of our relationships.

Second, the fruit of the Spirit that are restorative in nature restore our spiritual consciousness to vigor and health. When we are both conscious and healthy on spiritual things, we always respond properly. These fruit restore confidence, self-esteem, trust, dependence, and more; they restore a proper attitude and outlook on life. They are joy, *chara*; peace, *eirene*; and faith, *pistis*.

The fruit of the Spirit is joy. Joy is something that should be permanent in the heart of the Christian, no matter what the circumstances. The admonition to rejoice is found seventy times in the New Testament. Seventy times it says that Christians should rejoice, and yet Christians have long faces and sad attitudes. Why? Because we do not allow the Spirit to abide in us. The fruit of the Spirit is joy. Have you ever searched the Scriptures to see what they say about joy, rejoicing, and being joyful? Jesus says, "These things I have spoken to you so that My joy may be in you, and that your joy may be made full" (John 15:11). In Job, we find that "all the sons of God shouted for joy" (38:7). The psalmist praises God saying, "In Your presence is fullness of joy" (Ps 16:11). The prophet Habakkuk tells us, "I will rejoice in the God of my salvation" (3:18).

There is a difference between pleasure and joy. Pleasure depends on circumstances, but joy is independent of health or circumstances. You can lose health, wealth, and position and still have joy. "Joy is like a well containing sweet water." This is why the psalmist wrote, "There is a river, the streams whereof make glad the city of God" (Ps 46:4) Again he says, "My soul shall rejoice in the Lord" (Ps 35:9). It is to that end that Peter writes, "Rejoice with joy inexpressible and full of glory" (1 Pet 1:8). Joy rescues the spirit of the Christian. The joy that is the fruit of the Spirit is a lasting joy. "There is nothing I can give you which you have not, but there is much that while I cannot give you, you can take. The gloom of the world is but a shadow; behind it, yet within reach is joy, take joy."

The fruit of the Spirit is peace, *eirene*. What is peace? Peace has a positive existence. There are millions of people in the world who would gladly give their right hand, or anything for that matter, to find peace. You make a lot of money, you have sexual experiences, you get drunk, you acquire fame and knowledge, you accumulate wealth and a host of things, but you do not have peace. Your life is like an angry sea. Longfellow, the poet, echoed such dismay when he wrote, "And in despair I bowed my head; 'There is no peace on earth,' I said. 'For hate is strong and mocks the song of peace on earth, good will to men!'"[1]

The apostle Paul admonishes us when he says, "Let the peace of Christ rule in your hearts" (Col 3:15). Christ says, "My peace I give to you" (John 14:27). The peace that passes understanding comes to us when we yield to Christ and the Holy Spirit makes His abode in us. Yielding to the Spirit produces peace in our hearts in spite of the circumstances that surround us.

The fruit of the spirit is faithfulness (Greek *pistis*), sometimes called "trustworthiness" or "fidelity." Many English versions translate the word as faith in the Galatians 5 list of spiritual fruit. Strong's concordance defines it as "the character of one who can be relied on." The Greek Septuagint uses this word in

---

1. "I Heard the Bells on Christmas Day," Henry W. Longfellow, 1864.

Proverbs 28:20, which says, "A faithful man will abound with blessings."

Since the same word is translated elsewhere in the New Testament as faith, it's important to distinguish between the two. Hebrews 11:6 says, "Without faith it is impossible to please Him, for he who comes to God must believe that He is and that he is a rewarder of those who seek Him." Paul says that such faith comes from hearing the message of the gospel (Rom 10:17). Jesus challenged his hearers to "have faith in God" (Mark 11:22). Indeed, the Gospels often describe crowds of people who put their faith in Christ (e.g., John 8:30–31); these were not believers who had been filled with the Holy Spirit, but unbelievers who trusted Christ for their salvation as a result of hearing the Word of God.

But faithfulness appears in a believer's life through the work of the Holy Spirit. Revelation 13:10 says that the trials and persecutions of the last days will require "patient endurance and faithfulness on the part of the saints" (NIV). This is not faith (an unbeliever's ability to trust God for salvation through Christ); it is faithfulness (the character trait of a believer who remains loyal and true to God, no matter what happens). This Christlike trait can be produced only by the Holy Spirit living within us. The Holy Spirit produces within us the fruit of faithfulness, the ability to be obedient and live in holy conformity to God's will.

The third set of fruit of the Spirit are protective in nature. This means that they keep us sound and sober in the straight and narrow way spiritually. These fruit of the Spirit are goodness, kindness, and self-control. The King James translates *chrestotes* as "kindness," *agathosune* as "gentleness," and *egkrateia* as temperance (self-control). This fruit of the Spirit protects us and helps us maintain our spiritual equilibrium.

The fruit of the Spirit is kindness, *chrestotes*. This word means usefulness, profitable. Kindness is the grace that influences our whole nature; it is the mellowing of all which could be harsh. Kindness has to do with our whole disposition. Paul says that in the ages to come, God will "show the surpassing riches of His grace in kindness toward us in Christ Jesus" (Eph 2:7).

The fruit of the Spirit is goodness, *agathosune*. This is active goodness in our life, not just good deeds. Goodness is the mixture of every quality brought together, and it shines out in our life. It has to do with disposition and character. The word *goodness* refers to a particular quality of character. It is the character that expresses itself in active goodness. Paul prays for the Thessalonians that God "will fulfill every desire for goodness and the work of faith with power" (2 Thess 1:11). The psalmist says, "The goodness of God endures continually" (Ps 52:1 NKJV).

The fruit of the Spirit is self-control, *egkrateia*. The word means to be content, temperate, to have self-control or having power over. It means to be self-governing. It is the power to control ourselves and keep the body under subjection. *Egkrateia*, or self-control, means to be able to keep in check our thoughts, our appetites, our feelings, our actions, and our reactions, to be able to say no to ourselves, even on things that are good but not necessary.

The best evidence that we are indeed Christians, the best evidence that we have yielded to the Holy Spirit, is to have the fruit of the Spirit in our lives. The fruit of the Spirit, says Paul, are love, joy, peace, patience, kindness, goodness, faithfulness, gentleness, and self-control. Is the fruit of the Spirit evident in our lives? God wants us to live and walk in the Spirit so that His fruit will be obvious to others.

4. Steps toward Sanctification

We have seen that holiness is God's standard for His people. Sanctification is the will of God for every believer. The Bible admonishes us to seek "holiness, without which no one will see the Lord" (Heb 12:14 NKJV), and the expressed will of God is to "be holy; for I am holy" (1 Pet 1:16, citing Lev 11:44). We seek validation of this truth within the pages of the Holy Bible, and we must be unapologetically committed to follow its instruction. We must live with the determination and faith of John Wesley, who said, "I am determined to be a Bible Christian, not almost, but altogether. Who will meet me on this ground?"

Through the centuries, the experience of sanctification has been described by various terms, but the meaning has been consistent: It is our encounter with the fullness of the Holy Spirit, so that we experience freedom from sin, power over temptation and a transformation of our disposition toward God and man. Here are some of the phrases that Christian writers have used to describe such an experience: "The Rest of Faith"; "Resting in God"; "The Fullness of God"; "Holiness"; "Perfect Love"; "The Baptism with the Holy Spirit"; "Entire Sanctification; "Christian Perfection"; and "Full Consecration". These all describe various aspects of the work of the Holy Spirit in the heart of the believer that result in the experience of sanctification.

Holiness is indeed the central idea of Christianity. Liturgical symbolism and ritual, combined with the disciplines of Christian devotion, are intended to impress upon God's people that only those who have "pure hearts and clean hands" can approach the throne of God.

The majority of Christians hold that sanctification is a Bible doctrine that includes freedom from sin, accomplished through the merits of Christ's death, which is the rightful heritage of all those who are believers in Christ. The doctrine of sanctification began to be articulated by the church fathers, including Ignatius, Polycarp, Clement, and Augustine. This teaching was developed by the later mystics and Arminians; then it was fully developed by the Pietists, especially John and Charles Wesley. The Wesleyan teaching of sanctification gave rise to the Holiness Movement, of which the Church of God reformation movement is a part.

We noted earlier that even though most Christians hold to the truth of sanctification, they differ widely as to its nature, its time of attainment, and its outcome. These differences are largely due to different understandings of certain biblical terms.

Some Christians believe that sanctification begins in the experience of justification. Others claim that it takes place at the time of regeneration, while still others hold that sanctification is not really achieved until physical death. Christians of the Holiness Movement generally hold that sanctification takes place subsequent to regeneration as a crisis experience in which the believer yields to the fullness of the Spirit and is sanctified "entirely" (1 Thess 5:23).

Crucial to our understanding is the definition of sin. Is it a "willful transgression of the known will of God," or is it anything that falls short of the perfection of God?

The subject is further complicated by our different understandings of "self nature," "carnal nature," or "human nature." To what extent does the Holy Spirit change this nature of the believer? Does He eradicate or suppress it? How then should we interpret the scriptural admonition "lay aside the old self…and put on the new self" (Eph 4:22–24)? And how can we follow Peter's exhortation to "become partakers of the divine nature" (1 Pet 1:4)?

To be sure, the subject is complex and there are no easy answers. But one thing is certain: The Bible clearly teaches believers should be filled with the Spirit (Eph 5:18) and sanctified entirely (1 Thess 5:23), presenting their bodies as living sacrifices to God (Rom 12:1). Paul tells us that the believer, having been set free from sin (Rom 6:22), is to be conformed to the image of Christ (Rom 8:29) and walk in newness of life (Rom 6:4).

All of these admonitions are addressed to believers like us, subsequent to the experience of conversion, in order to move us toward growth, maturity, and perfection. Let us examine several biblical texts to discern the steps by which one enters into the experience of sanctification, and then seek to understand how sanctification is manifested in the daily life of the believer.

A careful study of the Bible both the Old and New Testaments confirms that holiness is God's desire and plan for His people. The New Testament indicates that it is a crisis experience in the life of the believer, the result of a personal encounter with the Holy Spirit in which the soul is delivered from the inner conflict of our human will with the divine will, cleansed and empowered to enjoy the likeness of Christ. Such a teaching in the New Testament presupposes the need for such a transformation in the life of the believer. Jesus admonished His disciples to wait in the city of Jerusalem until they had received "what the Father had promised" (Acts 1:4). Then he informed them of the outcome: "You will receive power when the Holy Spirit has come upon you" (Acts 1:8).[1]

The New Testament teaches that it is the will of God for His people to be sanctified: "So then do not be foolish, but understand what the will of the Lord is. And do not get drunk

---

1. Even though the totality of the redemptive grace of God rests on the merits of the death of Christ on the cross, the Holy Spirit is the agent of sanctification.

with wine, for that is dissipation, but be filled with the Spirit" (Eph 5:17–18). Paul addresses the Thessalonian Christians with the same conviction, "For this is the will of God, your sanctification; that is, that you abstain from sexual immorality" (1 Thess 4:3). Paul had earlier expressed his desire for them "to increase and abound in love for one another" and he prayed that the Holy Spirit "may establish your hearts without blame in holiness before our God" (1 Thess 3:12–13). Paul promises the believers in Thessaloniki that there is a definite experience that God wills for them that would impact the totality of their lives: "Now may the God of peace Himself sanctify you entirely; and may your spirit and soul and body be preserved complete, without blame at the coming of our Lord Jesus Christ. Faithful is He who calls you, and He also will bring it to pass" (1 Thess 5:23–24). There are two key Greek terms here: First, we have the aorist verb *hagiasai*, which punctuates the action, signifying action that occurs in a moment, a crisis. Second, we have the word *holoteleis*, which denotes an action that is entire, complete, through and through, an action that affects the whole soul, spirit, and body. This action makes the heart wholly holy.

God not only wills but also promises to sanctify His people. "'Come now, and let us reason together,' says the LORD, 'though your sins are as scarlet, they will be as white as snow; though they are red like crimson, they will be like wool'" (Is 1:18). "Then I will sprinkle clean water on you, and you will be clean; I will cleanse you from all your filthiness and from all your idols. Moreover, I will give you a new heart and put a new spirit within you; and I will remove the heart of stone from your flesh and give you a heart of flesh" (Ezek 36:25–26). Malachi the prophet emphasizes the cleansing aspect of this promise when he says, "But who can endure the day of His coming? And who can stand when He appears? For He is like a refiner's fire and like fullers' soap. He will sit as a smelter and purifier of silver, and He will purify the sons of Levi and refine them like gold and silver, so that they may present to the LORD offerings in righteousness" (Mal 3:2–3). John the Baptist seals the promise with these words: "As for me, I baptize you with water for repentance, but He who is coming after me is mightier than I, and I am not fit to remove His sandals; He will baptize you with the Holy Spirit and fire" (Matt 3:11).

To the will of God and the promise of God concerning our sanctification is added the commandment of God. He commands us to be holy: "You shall be holy, for I am holy" (1 Pet 1:16, quoting from Lev 11:44). And again: "Now when Abram was ninety-nine years old, the LORD appeared to Abram and said to him, 'I am God almighty; walk before Me and be blameless'" (Gen 17:1).

Scripture repeatedly declares that God's people need to be sanctified and that their prescribed behavior be characterized by holiness. "Having these promises, beloved, let us cleanse ourselves from all defilement of flesh and spirit, perfecting holiness in fear of God" (2 Cor 7:1). "If anyone cleanses himself from these things, he will be a vessel for honor, sanctified, useful to the Master, prepared for every good work" (2 Tim 2:21). "And now I commend you to God and to the word of His grace, which is able to build you up and to give you the inheritance among all those who are sanctified" (Acts 20:32). "...that they may receive forgiveness of sins and an inheritance among those who have been sanctified by faith in Me" (Acts 26:18).

So essential is the sanctification of God's people that the Lord Jesus Christ made it a matter of His high priestly prayer in John 17: "Sanctify them in the truth. Your word is truth...For their sakes I sanctify Myself, that they themselves also may be sanctified in truth. I do not ask on behalf of these alone, but for those also who believe in Me through their word" (vv 17, 19–20). Such scriptures convict and convince us that, as the people of God, we stand in need of an encounter with the Holy Spirit that will result in the sanctification of the soul and express itself in holiness of life. Such an encounter drastically transforms us, as we see in the case of the Ephesian elders (Acts 19:2–6), the experience of the Samaritan believers (Acts 8:14–24), and the experience in the house of Cornelius (Acts 10:44–48).

We may accept that sanctification is a Bible doctrine and we even may agree that it is the will of God for our life, but what does it mean in biblical terms to be sanctified? What is the nature of sanctification? What does sanctification do in our life, and when does it take place? You see, if we only understand the truth and neglect the experience, we will probably become dogmatic and hard. If we take only the experience and ignore the truth, we will probably become sentimental. But if we take them both as provided by the grace of God, we have authentic spiritual power and transformation. Truth plus experience equals spiritual power.

The Bible states that "all have sinned and fall short of the glory of God" (Rom 3:23) but that "if we confess our sins, He is faithful and righteous to forgive us our sins and to cleanse us from all unrighteousness" (1 John 1:9). We are all sinners. We were born sinners, and we chose to become sinners by breaking the laws of God. That makes us guilty before God. When we come to Christ through repentance and faith, God forgives our sins by the merits of the shed blood of Christ on the cross; thus, we are forgiven and justified before God. The penalty of our sin has been cancelled and we stand righteous before God. Then by the work of the Holy Spirit we are born from above or born again. We are regenerated or changed by the power of God and become partakers of divine life in its infancy. This experience of regeneration brings such a change in our lives that Paul describes it in these words: "If anyone is in Christ, he is a new creature; the old things passed away; behold, new things have come" (2 Cor 5:17). As born-again children of God, we endeavor to serve and please God in all things.

But it is the unanimous testimony of the Scriptures and the belief of the church throughout the centuries that the "original sin" or "inherited sin" (what John Wesley called our "inward sin") continues in the life of the believer until it is removed by the baptism of the Holy Spirit. This is the human instinct or natural tendency to sin. Sanctification cleanses the human heart from sin and God's indwelling presence empowers the believer for godly life and service. Sanctification delivers the soul from its inner conflict and grants us rest in the presence of God. It takes place once the believer becomes aware of the need and cries to God in faith and surrender, yielding fully to the Spirit.

Christian thinkers have made countless efforts to define and redefine "original sin". It is commonly agreed that it resulted from our loss of the moral image of God in the fall, which left us with the instinct or tendency to sin. The resulting "carnal nature" continues to cause conflict in the life of the believer. This carnal nature can be changed only by a crisis experience, commonly called the baptism of the Holy Spirit, a second work of grace, or entire sanctification. The experience of salvation is not compartmentalized but is one work as is indicated by the Greek word *soteria* (salvation), a word which literally means "to make whole, complete or healthy." The work of salvation is one in its totality; it encompasses justification, regeneration, sanctification, and our glorification after physical death. The grace of God progresses in our lives in pace with our awareness of our need and on the conditions of our faith, obedience, and yielding to God's will.

The Bible definitely calls us to sanctification by employing the related Greek words *hagios* (holy), *hagiasmos* (sanctification), *hagiosune* and *hagiotes* (holiness), and *hagiazo* (to sanctify; to make holy). All of these words have a twofold meaning. First, they indicate something or someone set apart for a particular use, as in the case of the vessels in the temple. These temple vessels were dedicated to be used exclusively for God's worship; any other use constituted defilement. In this sense, the words may be translated as "consecrate" or "consecration," as with

Jesus' declaration in John 17, "I sanctify myself," which could also be translated, "I consecrate myself."

Second, these words signify the altering of our inner attitudes or dispositions, which drastically transforms our behavior. Thus, the Bible always addresses its call for sanctification to believers. Writing to the Roman Christians, Paul admonishes them with these words: "I beseech you therefore brethren, by the mercies of God, that you present your bodies a living sacrifice, holy, acceptable unto God, which is your reasonable service. And do not be conformed to this world, but be transformed by the renewing of your mind, that you may prove what is that good and acceptable and perfect will of God" (Rom 12:1–2 NKJV). Paul's prayer for the Thessalonians—"Now may the God of peace Himself sanctify you entirely" (1 Thess 5:23)— is consistent with the prayer of our Lord for His disciples: "Sanctify them in the truth; Your word is truth" (John 17:17).

It should be noticed that in the three above references: ("present your bodies"; "sanctify you entirely"; and "sanctify them in the truth"), the aorist tense is used, which signifies a momentary act that does not lose its effect over time. "Sanctify them" (aorist imperative) means an instantaneous work in the heart of the believer that happens once for all.

We should note that sanctification is not freedom from temptation or freedom from the possibility of sin, but freedom from the will to sin. It does not alter the basic drives of the human nature, but it does bring them under the subjection of the Holy Spirit to the extent that spirit, soul, and body can live blameless before God.

The questions remain, How and when can such an experience take place, and what kind of steps of preparation should one follow? Sanctification is not an arbitrary gift that God bestows upon us. God responds to the hunger and pursuit of the human heart; thus we are admonished to seek and believe for sanctification.

Our preparation begins with an awareness of the need and a general dissatisfaction with the inner condition and our lack of progress in the effort to live a holy life. Such awareness becomes painful and causes the heart to cry for help.

Second, there is an intense hunger and the desire for spiritual transformation. The longing heart becomes willing to pay any price and go any distance to achieve victory over sin and to enjoy the inner rest of God.

I recall such an intense hunger in my own soul soon after I came to Christ at the age of fifteen. The hunger and the struggle were so intense that I engaged in all sorts of spiritual disciplines, to no avail. Then at the age of seventeen I found myself in the presence of a white-haired man of God whose disposition and life were the epitome of the fullness of the Spirit. In the presence of two other men (who were resistant to the truth), he introduced me to the fullness of the Spirit and in a matter of moments led me step by step in the most powerful encounter with the Spirit. As I responded, instantaneously I found inner rest and freedom from the struggle compounded with the spiritual power to say no to temptation without any reluctance. Not only do we need to desire this transformation, but we also need to pray for and seek such an encounter with the Spirit. "These all with one mind were continually devoting themselves to prayer" (Acts 1:14). The outcome of such an effort is the fullness of the Spirit as described in Acts 2:1–4.

Third, the believer must make a complete surrender to the whole will of God for time and eternity. It is to this end that the apostle Paul admonishes us to "present your bodies a living and holy sacrifice, acceptable to God." Nothing is kept off of the altar–talents, gifts, dreams, aspirations, or the whole life itself. This act of consecration opens the door for the baptism of the Holy Spirit and thus the experience of sanctification.

Fourth, all the graces of God (merits from the death of Christ on the cross) are incorporated into our life by faith. "You have been saved," says the scripture, "through faith"

(Eph 2:8). Further, "without faith it is impossible to please [God]" (Heb 11:6). Without faith none of the benefits of redemption will affect our life. By faith we experience forgiveness of sin and receive the gifts of God's grace in our life.

In fact, faith and consecration are interwoven together. There is no consecration without faith, and without faith we cannot receive the cleansing, empowering gift of the Spirit. Faith is the key to every door of grace. Paul affirms that the blessing of the infilling of the Holy Spirit is received by faith: "I have been crucified with Christ; and it is no longer I who live, but Christ lives in me; and the life which I now live in the flesh I live by faith in the Son of God, who loved me and gave Himself up for me" (Gal 2:20). Further, Peter says, God "made not distinction between us and them [Jewish and Gentile Christians], cleansing their hearts by faith" (Acts 15:9).

So entire sanctification delivers us from the carnal nature. It puts the human nature in subjection to the will of God. It frees us from the will to sin, although we are still subject to temptation and the possibility of sin. It not only cleanses us, but also empowers us for holy living and service. It is received by the believer subsequent to conversion by an act of consecration and faith. It is received in an instantaneous work of the Holy Spirit, although it is preceded and followed by spiritual growth that lasts a lifetime. We always grow in grace, knowledge, and wisdom.

What then are some of the practical consequences for those who have received the fullness of the Spirit? Such an experience frees us from pride and self-centeredness and adorns us with the spirit of humility. This changes our tempers, dispositions, attitudes, and emotions. Holiness is expressed as a disposition of mind and spirit that bears fruit in behavior.

In an article titled "Holiness for the 21st Century," Dr. Brian D. Russell states, "There is a burning in our day to recapture scriptural holiness."[2] Then he moves on to state five applications of holiness in our life today.

First, holiness involves *character transformation*. A holy life reflects God's character. It is Christlikeness. It is the work of the Holy Spirit to restore us to the kind of people that God created us to be. This character transformation not only changes our external behavior but also represents a deep inward cleansing of our motives and priorities, which prepares us for full and active participation in God's mission in the world.

Second, holiness leads us into a *commissioned life*. Holiness cannot be separated from the mission of God. We are sanctified and sent. God has saved us from the world, but we remain in the world so that we can serve as Jesus' witnesses to and for the world. Holiness is not merely about our relationship with God; it enables our witness in and for the world. God desires to sanctify us so that we can be deployed fully for God's Great Commission.

Third, holiness will lead us into a *communal life*. God's people are to be a holy community. Holiness is lived out in our authentic relationship with others. Holiness helps us to discover the unity of the church and rediscover the power of the church as the body of Christ. The sanctifying power of God helps us to maintain the unity of the Spirit and motivates us to love and value each other in the body of Christ.

Fourth, holiness will give us a *contextual ministry*. That means that the Spirit of Christ teaches us to encourage lost people in ways relevant to their particular culture. Paul not only exemplified such an approach but also he stated it clearly for all of us: "I have become all things to all men, so that I may by all means save some" (1 Cor 9:22). God's call for holiness of heart and life is transcultural and is valid for all people.

Fifth, holiness will give us a *courageous ministry*. Jesus' call to discipleship is radical: "If anyone wishes to come after Me, he must deny himself, and take up his cross and follow Me"

---

2. *The Asbury Herald* 117, no. 2 (2007): 10.

(Matt 16:24). Holiness in our time is a courageous way of life in which Christ's followers engage the world with the gospel with a vigor and a vitality that come only from a Spirit-driven deep relationship with God. This is why it is essential for us as modern-day disciples to have "a high-altitude-Spirit-drenched encounter with the living God that will propel us to holy living and a courageous engagement in God's mission."[3]

3. Ibid., 10–11.

5. The Universal Quest for Holiness

Every human heart desires moral purity and a sense of peace in the inner self. The quest is evident in every religion, from ancient Judaism to Hinduism, from Islam to the New Age cults, from Catholicism to Eastern Orthodoxy, and in every sort of Protestant group from Baptists to Presbyterians, and from Methodists to Church of God people.

Never mind if some prescriptions for the quest are wrong or the means at times complex and meaningless to us. The truth of the matter is that while every heart is prone to evil, at the same time it has the capacity for good and it desires freedom and purity. Let us consider various attempts to find holiness, setting aside for a moment the question of whether their quests are valid.

People have used extreme disciplines in their quest for the purification of the soul. Some have made untold sacrifices and have traveled immeasurable distances. Religion has instituted an incredible array of cultic practices and observances for the same purpose. Some seekers after holiness will kill what they call "the infidel," with the belief that such an act will open the gates of heaven for them. (While it is easy to reject such a perception as erroneous and deceptive, the desire for spiritual perfection is nonetheless what drives certain religious groups to do these things. Some believe these acts of zealotry will assure them of achieving their spiritual goal, while others can only hope without any certainty of the outcome.)

Scholars of comparative religion observe that every great religion seeks to experience the divine, the holy, or the other. But without any revelation of who that divine being is and without any understanding of who man is and how he has come to be in this world, the various religions have devised their own disciplines and spiritual paths.

It is not my aim here to get entangled in the complex study of comparative religion but simply to note that the quest for purity and peace is universal. There is a vacuum in all of us that cannot be filled with anything else except the divine. But how do we experience the divine? Man is incapable of experiencing or being conformed to the divine without a revelation. This is where we get the real distinction between other religions and the Christian faith. While other religions urge individuals to search for the divine, the Christian faith holds that God has revealed Himself to mankind in an indisputable way.

The Bible begins with the words, "In the beginning God..." It then proceeds to tell us how the Spirit of God moved upon a creation that was "formless" and how He spoke light into existence and divided it from the darkness.

The evangelist John begins his gospel with the word: "In the beginning was the Word, and the Word was with God, and the Word was God." John then tells us who this God is, what He is, and what He does. John tells us that this God reveals Himself to us in tangible ways so that we can see, hear, and feel him. This sovereign God, who is self-existing and self-sufficient and who has all power and all knowledge, reveals Himself in the finite, temporal world.

Simple observation of the marvels of creation will fill the heart with awe of how great, wise, powerful, just, righteous, loving, merciful, and holy the Creator God is. Stand at the brightness of a sunrise and behold the beauty of a sunset; endeavor to comprehend the vastness of this universe and how infinite God is. Only a fool will conclude this universe just happened. God made everything, and it all declares the glory and the majesty of God.

The Bible tells us that God made humankind. "God created man in His own image, in the image of God He created him; male and female He created them" (Gen 1:27). Then the Bible tells us that God breathed into the nostrils of this creature and he became a living soul. Many ideas are suggested by the expression the "image of God." It certainly does not mean that the appearance of the human body resembles God or vice versa, even though Scripture often uses anthropological characteristics to describe God.

Mildred Bangs Wynkoop and others have defined the image of God as our capacity for loving relationships. H. Ray Dunning elaborates by speaking of our relationships with God, others, ourselves, and the earth."[1] I believe the "image of God" refers to the capacity of humanity, given by God, to love others as God loves and to be conformed to the moral and spiritual nature of God. Adam Clark says, "This has reference not to the body of man but to his soul—his mind, soul, must have been formed after the nature and perfection of his God." He further states, "God is holy, just, wise, good and perfect: so must the soul be that springs from Him. There could be in him nothing impure, unjust, ignorant, evil, and low base, mean or vile."[2] Paul alludes to this image when he talks about the "new self" that is "created in righteousness and holiness of the truth" (Eph 4:24) and is "renewed to a true knowledge according to the image of the One who created him" (Col 3:10).

The women and men whom God thus created for His pleasure and His glory had all the potential to be conformed to the moral nature of God; to function with the capacity to love and relate fully to God, to others and to themselves; and to be motivated and made capable for every work of faithful service by the imprint of their Creator upon them. This man and

---

1. Diane LeClerc, "Holiness: Sin's Anticipated Cure," in *The Holiness Manifesto*, ed. Kevin W. Mannoia and Don Thorsen, 110–126 (Grand Rapids, MI: William B. Eerdmans, 2008).

2. Adam Clark, *The Holy Bible*, vol. 1, (Nashville: Abingdon Press, [1977]), 36.

woman were placed in the garden of Eden, where everything was permeated by the nature of God. Thus, Adam and Eve enjoyed perfect fellowship, perfect Communion, and perfect relationship with God. They were wise, holy, and righteous. The provisions of the garden were adequate for them in order to please and glorify God.

Adam and Eve had two responsibilities in the garden: One was "to cultivate it and to keep it" (Gen 2:15). The other was to refrain from eating of the tree of the knowledge of good and evil "for in the day that you eat from it you will surely die" (Gen 2:17). There is no need here to discuss the nature of the tree, because the destiny of humanity did not rest upon the nature of the tree but upon the fidelity of their obedience to the command of God. They had mastery over the garden and the earth so long as they remained under the lordship of a sovereign God.

The whole future of God's relationship with humanity rested on these words: "but from the tree of the knowledge of good and evil you shall not eat" (Gen 1:17). But they did eat from that tree, they did disobey God, and the tragic outcome is painted with vivid colors in the pages of the Bible: fellowship with God was lost; God's trust was broken; the intent of God for humanity was interrupted; sin was born; and alienation from God became the human condition.

The sin of disobedience brings separation, pain, exclusion from the holy environment of the Garden, confusion, and misdirection in life. The disobedience of the first couple led the whole human race down the tragic path of despair and hopelessness, missing the "image of God" and lacking His peace.

Theologians have long debated whether the image of God was obliterated by the fall or simply obscured. Is the depravity of humanity total or does there remain some good in each of us, leaving us with the capability to do good? Whatever your answer to these questions, the fact remains that fallen humanity immediately began to reap the wages of their sinful disobedience, and ever since that time we stand in need of redemption.

The sovereign God who took the initiative to make humanity now took the initiative for our redemption. The redemptive initiative of God is revealed in two ways in the garden. First, we hear it in the words of God that the seed of the woman will bruise the serpent's head. Second, we see it in God's provision of skins to clothe Adam and Eve, which implies that the sacrifice or death of living creatures had occurred. So in the garden we have the introduction of hamartiology (the nature and the effects of sin) and soteriology (the promise and the means for salvation).

But God had a plan for the redemption of mankind and provided laws in order to restore the fallen human nature. The plan of God—which involved the coming of a redeemer or savior—was communicated through symbols, types, rituals, and prophetic predictions of the coming Messiah, who would be called Emmanuel (God with us). Hundreds of years passed before the time was right for God to send His Son to redeem the fallen human race. "For God so loved the world, that He gave His only begotten Son, that whoever believes in Him shall not perish, but have eternal life" (John 3:16).

Christ was born of a virgin, lived a sinless life, died on a cross, and was raised from the dead in order to redeem us so that we can walk in newness of life. This is why the apostle Paul says: "For I delivered to you as of first importance what I also received, that Christ died for our sins according to the Scriptures, and that He was buried, and that he was raised on the third day according to the Scriptures" (1 Cor 15:3–4). Elsewhere, he also says: "For the grace of God has appeared, bringing salvation to all men, instructing us to deny ungodliness and worldly desires to live sensibly, righteously, and godly in the present age, looking for the blessed hope and the appearing of the glory of our great God and Savior, Christ Jesus, who gave

Himself for us to redeem us from every lawless deed, and to purify for Himself a people for His own possession, zealous for good deeds" (Titus 2:11–14).

Two phrases in this second passage merit our attention: "to redeem us" and "to purify for Himself a people for His own possession." The aim of God in redemption is to have a holy people for Himself. The salvation provided by the grace of God, through Christ, encompasses the totality of our deliverance from sin and our restoration to God. So before we talk about the gift of holiness, the process of holiness, and the experience of holiness in the life of the believer, we must clearly understand the nature of *hamartia* (sin), its root, and its fruit, which we have inherited and perpetuated by our actions. We have inherited the nature, the instinct, and the inclination to sin, but we brought it to fruition by committing acts of sin, such as lying, coveting, and lusting. We are not personally responsible for the instinct to sin, but we are responsible for yielding and following that instinct.

Sin is *anomia* (lawlessness, the willful transgression of the law). It is disobedience to the Word of God. It is saying no to the will of God. It is missing the mark, veering aside from the intent or the purpose of God. So we have the nature of sin ("inbred sin" or "the Adamic nature," as it is called by some) and we have committed acts of sin, acts which we willfully committed knowing that they violated the law of God. Holiness must deal with both levels of sin and provide deliverance, cleansing, and restoration whereby we regain the relationship God intended for us to have with him so that we can live unashamedly in His presence.

We must think critically about the *apolytrosis* (redemptive work) of Christ. Every divine grace bestowed upon us, every victory won, every change that takes place within the heart of a believer—whether it be deliverance, sanctification, empowerment, or moral transformation—all rest upon the death and resurrection of our Lord Jesus Christ. All are provided through the merit of His shed blood on the cross of Calvary. Consider all that His blood does for us:

- We are purchased by His blood (Acts 20:28).
- We are justified by His blood (Rom 5:9).
- We have been brought near to God by His blood (Eph 2:13).
- We are redeemed by His blood (Col 1:14).
- We are forgiven of sin through His blood (Col 1:14).
- We have peace with God through His blood (Col 1:20).
- We are cleansed by His blood (Heb 9:14; 1 John 1:7).
- We are sanctified by His blood (Heb 13:12).
- We have been released from our sin by His blood (Rev 1:5).

So no spiritual merit or grace is bestowed upon us apart from the blood of Christ, including the experience of holiness. The words of the apostle Paul to the Ephesians impress this upon our minds: "Husbands, love your wives, just as Christ also loved the church and gave Himself up for her, so that He might sanctify her, having cleansed her by the washing of water with the word, that He might present to Himself the church in all her glory, having no spot or wrinkle or any such thing; but that she would be holy and blameless" (Eph 5:25–27).

Let us say a few words about the New Testament truth of *soteria* (salvation). Soteria refers to the redemptive plan of God; it encompasses all the grace and mercy of God to fully restore us and make us fit for heaven. The meaning of the word is wholeness, completeness, and health. It further means safety, preservation, and deliverance from danger. It means deliverance from sin (Jer 31:31–34), deliverance from the spiritual consequences of sin (Ps 5:10–12), and deliverance from future condemnation or the judgment of God (Rom 3:1). Salvation also means freedom from sin as a present power (2 Cor 5:17; Rom 6:2).

In describing the plan of salvation, Scripture also talks about justification. The apostle Paul says, "Therefore, having been justified by faith, we have peace with God" (Rom 5:1). The Greek word in the New Testament is *lutrosis* (to release or to set free, especially by paying a ransom). A related Greek word is *apolutrosis* (to let go, to free from captivity or slavery). The Bible presents sin as a kind of slavery and sinners as slaves (see John 8:34; Rom 6:17-18). "Everyone who commits sin is a slave of sin" (John 8:34). "But thanks be to God that though you were slaves of sin, you became obedient from the heart to that form of teaching to which you were committed" (Rom 6:17). Justification has the idea that our sin is forgiven, our debt has been cancelled, and our guilt has been removed through the death of Christ on the cross; therefore, we have peace with God and no longer live under the bondage of sin's condemnation. Justification denotes the forgiveness of sin we have committed and the restoration of our moral integrity before God, even though sin's consequences may persist for the rest of our earthly life.

The Bible's teaching of salvation also utilizes the word *regeneration*, which has the meaning of the old replaced by the new. The verb form of the word in the Greek New Testament is *anagennao*, which means "to beget again." This is the word used to describe the believer's status as a child of God (Col 3:26); one born of the Spirit (John 3:8); or one born again (John 3:3).

Another word used in the Greek New Testament for regeneration is the word *poliggenesia*. It is used in Titus 3:5 to describe the spiritual rebirth of the individual soul. Through this experience, an individual puts off the old sinful nature and puts on the new regenerated nature. This is, in the words of Paul, the one who lays "aside the old self with its evil practices" and has "put on the new self who is being renewed to a true knowledge according to the image of the One who created him" (Col 3:9–10). Wiley states, "Regeneration is that mighty change in man, wrought by the Holy Spirit, by which the dominion which sin had over him in his natural state, and which he deplores and struggles against in his penitent state, is broken and abolished; so that with full choice of will and the energy of right affections, he serves God freely, and runs in the way of His commandments."[3]

We cannot describe the redemptive work of Christ without making reference to the work of the Holy Spirit. The Holy Spirit's presence and influence are evident from the beginning of creation and throughout the dispensation of grace until the consummation of all things. Scripture says that the Holy Spirit is the administrator of the manifold grace of God (see 1 Pet. 4:10). The Holy Spirit both convicts and convinces, witnesses and guides, teaches and helps, gifts and purges, empowers and anoints—all in order to make us capable of conforming to the image of Christ and doing the will of God.

Conviction comes from the Holy Spirit. Repentance and faith in Christ are the work of the Holy Spirit. Neither justification nor regeneration can be effected in our lives without the assistance of the Holy Spirit. Sanctification and the life of holiness are the work of the Holy Spirit. Thus the Bible exhorts us to "be filled with the Spirit," to "walk in the Spirit," to "live in the Spirit," and to "pray in the Spirit." Then the Bible warns us not to "grieve the Spirit" (Eph 4:30) and not to "quench the Spirit." When the Holy Spirit makes His abode in us, we become the temple of God, purged from the dominion of sin, endowed with the perfect love of God, empowered to conform to the image of Christ, and anointed to be victorious in doing the will of God joyfully and eagerly.

The New Testament makes it clear that the work of the Holy Spirit in the life of the believer is indispensable. Without His assistance, we can neither pray effectively nor progress in the experience of holiness. In the process and experience of holiness, we find our best ally and enabler in the Holy Spirit,

---

3. H. Orton Wiley, *Christian Theology*, vol 2 (Kansas City, MO: Beacon Hill Press), 406–7.

"for the law of the Spirit of life in Christ Jesus has set you free from the law of sin and of death" (Rom 8:2).

The Bible's teaching about salvation and the lifelong journey of holiness also talks about self-denial, surrender, and consecration. The sinful self always appears in Scripture as a stumbling block to the intended purpose of God in our lives. Individualism and the demand for individual rights is not the ideal held before us by Scripture; rather, we are called to a life of humility and servanthood, yielding to the lordship of Christ so that He increases in our lives and we decrease.

We tend to avoid two words when we consider the process of salvation and the pursuit of holiness; but according to the New Testament, they are indispensable. These words are *brokenness* and *abandonment.* Brokenness incorporates repentance, contrition, and humility, relying wholly on the grace of God without putting confidence on any self merits. It is to that end that the psalmist states, "A broken and a contrite heart, O God, You will not despise" (Ps 51:17).

It is inconceivable that the Holy Spirit could dwell within us and effect holiness in our lives without our total abandonment to the grace of God and a total trust in His faithfulness. Jesus said that the key to genuine discipleship is for one to deny oneself. Paul says to Titus that the grace of God teaches "us to deny ungodliness and worldly desires" (Titus 2:12). Instructing the Roman Christians how to achieve nonconformity to this world and enter into the transformation of a renewed mind, Paul states, "present your bodies a living and holy sacrifice" (Rom 12:1).

The Greek word here is *thusia,* from the root word *thou* (to sacrifice). The word *thusia* refers to the sacrifice or offering that a worshiper abandoned at the altar of God. The only limit to the extent of holiness in our lives and usefulness in the kingdom of God, is the extent of our brokenness and self-abandonment for love's sake, the point at which Christ is all in all.

Sanctification (*hagiasmos* or *hagiosuni* in Greek) is an important part of the totality of our salvation. The Bible says it includes the will of God for our entire life, including the soul, mind, and body. The root word *hagios*, which means "set apart," "sanctified," "consecrated," or "saintly," has its root in *hagnos*, which means "chaste." "The fundamental idea," says Dr. Spiros Zodhiates, "is separation, consecration and/or devotion to the service of deity, sharing in God's purity and abstaining from earthly defilement. The word *hagios*, holy, means pure or ceremonially clean as well as morally pure. According to Romans 12:1, it means 'perfect without blemish, morally pure and blameless in heart and life.'"[4]

So, to experience sanctification is to be set aside as God's for His exclusive use. The New Testament term makes clear that sanctification is the work of the Holy Spirit: "God has chosen you from the beginning for salvation through sanctification by the Spirit and faith in the truth" (2 Thess 2:13). Sanctified believers are "chosen according to the foreknowledge of God the Father, by the sanctifying work of the Spirit, to obey Jesus Christ and be sprinkled with His blood" (1 Pet 1:2). So sanctification is an entire separation of the life to God with an instant cleansing by the Holy Spirit which effects holiness in our lives with progressive changes.

The word *hagiosune* (holiness) is a quality of character and appears only three times in the New Testament:

a. Romans 1:4. "Who was declared the Son of God with power by the resurrection from the dead, according to the Spirit of holiness, Jesus Christ our Lord." This refers to the holiness of God.

b. 2 Corinthians 7:1. "Therefore, having these promises, beloved, let us cleanse ourselves from all defilement of the flesh and spirit, perfecting holiness in the fear of

---

4. Spiros Zodhiates, *The Complete Wordstudy New Testament* (Chattanooga, TN: AMG Publishers, 1971), 70.

God." Here we have an exhortation to the believer to endeavor to perfect holiness or to live a victorious life in the fear of God.

c. 1 Thessalonians 3:13. "So that He may establish your hearts without blame in holiness before our God and Father at the coming of our Lord Jesus Christ with all His saints." Here Paul speaks of the holiness of man, a life that is well pleasing to God. Ephesians 1:4 confirms that God has chosen us before the foundation of the world to be holy. Colossians 1:22 says that it was God's intent through the death of Christ "to present [us] holy and blameless and beyond reproach."

One more New Testament word describes the gateway to all the grace of God and all the benefits of salvation. That word is *metanoia* (repentance). Scripture states that "God is now declaring to men that all people everywhere should repent" (Acts 17:30) and that such repentance is a turning toward God (20:21). Now *metanoia* has to do with change of direction, not merely a change of mind, and it is enabled by the Spirit of God. It is a change of attitude and disposition, as well as the change of life purpose. It is a change from evil to good and from good to better. "Therefore bear fruit in keeping with repentance" (Matt 3:8). It is a humble contrition and godly sorrow toward God through which the individual is greatly troubled by the Spirit of God by seeing what has been done and what has been missed as a result of sin. Repentance is not just a single act but a state in which we always maintain a repentant attitude toward God.

Repentance is the brokenness of the human heart before God. Such brokenness leads to faith and proceeds to the experience of salvation, the infilling of the Holy Spirit, and a life of holiness. In fact, the brokenness of repentance is essential for revival or spiritual renewal.

In repentance we say, "I am deeply sorry for trusting in myself, seeking my way, and I change my mind. I fully abandon myself in the hands and mercy of God and fully trust in His faithfulness for the well-being of my soul."

A repentant attitude, energized by the Holy Spirit, is the gateway to every spiritual benefit offered to us by God. It is the path to spiritual awakening as well as to the progress of holiness of life. Repentance is always a move, prompted by the Holy Spirit, away from conformity to self and to the world and its spirit, toward conformity to the image of our Lord and Savior, Jesus Christ. As the children of God, we are not only challenged but "predestinated to become conformed to the image of His Son, so that He would be the firstborn among many brethren" (Rom 8:29). After all, the essence of holiness is having our lives conformed to the life of Jesus Christ, who "that He might sanctify the people through His own blood, suffered outside the gate" (Heb 13:12).

6. *The Biblical Doctrine of Holiness*

L et us now turn to the goal for which every true believer longs—that is, holiness of heart and life. Scripture introduces holiness as a way of life for all of God's people.

The Bible's teaching about holiness is both dogmatic and ethical. First, it is dogmatic because it gives attention to what is true (doctrine), presenting with urgency what one ought to believe. Christian faith is not just believing but believing the right thing. Life becomes misguided and confused when we lose faith in the truth. You see, what we believe gives us our identity. The doctrines that we believe are the glue that keeps us together.

The New Testament goes to some pains to make sure that we believe the right thing and that we are not carried away with every wind of doctrine or teaching (see Eph 4:14). When Jesus began to preach, it was the contrast of His doctrine (teaching) with that of the Pharisees that created the biggest uproar: "When the crowds heard this, they were astonished at His teaching" (Matt 22:33). Jesus made sure that people not only understood His doctrine but that they knew the authority behind it: "My teaching is not Mine, but His who sent me. If anyone is willing to do His will, he will know of the teaching, whether it is of God or whether I speak from Myself" (John 7:16–17).

The New Testament church put great emphasis on doctrine, and their doctrine was always translated into their experience.

Notice what Scripture says about the early church: "They were continually devoting themselves to the apostles' teaching and to fellowship, to the breaking of bread and to prayer" (Acts 2:42). Also notice how the apostle Paul admonished Timothy that church leaders were "not to teach strange doctrines" (1 Tim 1:3). He counseled this early pastor to be "nourished on the words of the faith and of the sound doctrine which you have been following" (4:6). "Until I come, give attention to the public reading of Scripture, to exhortation and teaching" (v 13). "Pay close attention to yourself and to your teaching; persevere in these things, for as you do this you will ensure salvation both for yourself and for those who hear you" (v 16). "The elders who rule well are to be considered worthy of double honor, especially those who work hard at preaching and teaching" (5:17). "If anyone advocates a different doctrine and does not agree with sound words, those of our Lord Jesus Christ, and with the doctrine conforming to godliness, he is conceited and understands nothing" (6:3–4).

The neglect of sound doctrine has grave consequence for the believer and the church. We are in danger of having a generation of Christians who are practically ignorant when it comes to the doctrine of holiness.

Second, the message of the Bible about holiness is ethical, which means that it endeavors to answer the question, What should we do? It is in this area that the message of holiness is most often expounded.

The ethics of the Bible deal with duties we owe to God, to others, to ourselves, and to the people of God. Scripture is unequivocal in describing the kind of behavior that characterizes disciples of Christ. The outward life of the Christian takes its character from the quality of the inner spiritual life.

The mandate of biblical holiness is unmistakably clear: "You shall be holy, for I am holy" (1 Pet 1:16, quoting Lev 11:44). Our relationship with God makes us partakers of the divine nature (2 Pet 1:4). Our response must be an active engagement in perfecting holiness in the fear of God. "Therefore, having these promises, beloved, let us cleanse ourselves from all defilement of flesh and spirit, perfecting holiness in fear of God" (2 Cor 7:1).

The writer of the book of Hebrews challenges us by saying, "Pursue peace with all people, and holiness, without which no one will see the Lord" (Heb 12:14). The mandate is clear: God is holy, so we must be holy people. How? By surrendering to divine grace and yielding to the Spirit of God so that we can be satisfied with nothing less than a life of total holiness. We will approach the subject under the following topics:

a. The *Perception* of Holiness. What are our thoughts?
b. The *Prescription* of Holiness. What must we do? What principles or disciplines do we follow?
c. The *Practice* of Holiness. What inward and outward changes take place and to what extent do others see behavioral changes in our lives?
d. The *Power* of Holiness. Enablement and benefits for the service of God.

The Perception of Holiness

The majority of God's people will wholeheartedly agree that God wants His people to be holy, that it is His will for Christ's disciples to be sanctified, and that He has foreordained us to be conformed to the image of His Son, Jesus Christ.

But we have differences in perception when it comes to our definitions of holiness. What is it? When does it happen? What does happen? How does it happen? And what is the outcome? What is the role of the Holy Spirit in the holy life, and what is our role in it?

Some Christians believe that holiness is a life of isolation from the world. They live reclusively, giving themselves to the discipline of fasting, prayer, and studying Scripture diligently with the hope that they will mortify the flesh and thus purify the soul. This perception was the basis of the monasticism

61

that grew in the medieval period as a reaction to the growing worldliness in the church. But Christ prayed that the Father would not take us out of the world, rather to keep us from the evil one while living in the world.

Other believers perceive that real holiness can be attained only after physical death. They say, "Yes, God commands us to be holy and we begin that process the moment that we are saved by the grace of God. When we gave our hearts to Christ, he sees us as being holy by virtue of our position in Christ. That is why we are called saints. But in this world we have a continuous struggle without complete victory over sin. It is only at death that we will experience perfect deliverance and victory over sin."

Another viewpoint was popularized by the Keswick Movement, which arose in England in the late nineteenth century. These Christians believe that the Holy Spirit is the agent of God's redeeming grace, that we receive Him at regeneration, and that we are sanctified by the Spirit. God then views us as holy and we begin to experience a progressive maturation in holiness, which they understand to be the meaning of sanctification. Adherents of the Keswick viewpoint believe that original sin or inbred sin is suppressed by the power of God, but we are never free from it. Well-known Bible commentator G. Campbell Morgan believes there is an initial sanctification in regeneration and "apart from it there cannot be final sanctification." He goes on to further state, "Sanctification, experientially, is a progressive relation, for not by an event of light and conscious blessing and consecration does any man come to maturity in the Christian character." Later he makes a statement in which he appears to contradict himself when he says, "Sanctification is a progressive exercise, it is gradual as well as sudden, that which is gradual results from that which is sudden; that which is sudden being the adjustment of the life to God and the immediate reception of the power."[1]

---

1. Clyde E. Fant, Jr., and William M. Pinson (eds.), *20 Centuries of Great Preaching*, vol. 8 (Waco, TX: Word Books, 1971), 25

Still other Christians believe that a Christian eventually becomes aware of the inner struggle, senses the need for divine intervention, and cries to God for cleansing and deliverance. This cleansing is a crisis experience in which the individual totally abandons or surrenders himself to God, trusting God for full deliverance from the influence of his sinful nature. As a result, the Holy Spirit comes to fully cleanse, deliver, and empower the believer for the journey of a holy life.

John Wesley once wrote a letter to a Roman Catholic in which he described the role of the Holy Spirit in such an experience. He wrote, "I believe the infinite and eternal Spirit of God, equal with the Father and the Son, to be not only perfectly holy in Himself, but the immediate cause of all holiness in us; enlightening our understanding, rectifying our wills and affections, renewing our natures, uniting our passions to Christ, assuring us of the adoption of sons, leading us in our actions, purifying and sanctifying our souls and bodies, to a full and eternal enjoyment of God."[2]

The Holiness Movement puts a great emphasis on the doctrine of "Christian perfection" or "entire sanctification" as it was articulated by John Wesley, who said that holiness is "perfection in love" as we abandon ourselves fully to the Holy Spirit and receive divine power over sin. The Holiness Movement defines holiness or sanctification as "A second crisis or blessing following conversion in which a high degree of consecration and sanctification takes place so that the believer is lifted to a new plane of spirituality and purity of intent that permitted a life of 'victory over sin.'"[3] Some Holiness people describe it as a "second blessing," which is the result of "the infilling of the Holy Spirit." They affirm that the call to scriptural holiness challenges every generation of believers, and they describe such an experience using various terms: "entire

---

2. Quoted in Alex R. G. Deasley and R. Larry Shelton, eds., *The Spirit of the New Age* (Anderson, IN: Warner Press, 1986), 254.

3. Ibid.

sanctification," "Christian perfection," "a second definite work of grace," "deliverance from embedded [or inbred] sin," and "purity of heart."

The Holiness Movement teaches that holiness is a present life experience that can be conferred by the grace of God through the power of the Holy Spirit when there is a complete consecration and surrender to God. It is both the intent and the will of God that all believers live a holy life in this world. In fact, as we noted earlier, the Bible tells us that God has predestined us to be conformed to the image of His Son Jesus Christ (Rom 8:29). By the grace of God, we can live a victorious life in this world, free from the power of sin.

The Prescription of Holiness

The Bible describes holiness as a way of life in which the Holy Spirit abides in us. As Jesus said, He will be in you. In such a relationship, we walk in the Spirit, live in the Spirit, and pray in the Spirit. As a result, the law of the Spirit has made us free from the law of sin (Rom 8:2). Such a relationship with the Spirit raises us to the level where we mind the things of the Spirit and we are spiritually motivated rather than carnally motivated.

The death of Christ on the cross was not only to save us from the guilt and penalty of sin, but also to deliver us from the ongoing power of sin. He sacrificed himself in order to sanctify a people to Himself. When Zacharias was filled with the Holy Spirit, he prophesied that God would "grant us that we, being rescued from the hand of our enemies, might serve Him without fear, in holiness and righteousness before Him all our days" (Luke 1:74–75).

It would be difficult to deny that the Bible prescribes holiness in all levels of our lives: holiness of heart, holiness of life, holiness in disposition, and even holiness of body. In other words, holiness is a holistic relationship with God, with others, with ourselves, and with the world.

First, the Bible prescribes that holiness should characterize our relationship with God. God is holy and we are commanded to love this holy God with all our soul, mind, and strength. How do we do that? By responding to His love. The apostle Peter tells us that the promises of God were given to us in order to achieve union with God through holiness: "For by these He has granted to us His precious and magnificent promises, so that by them you may become partakers of the divine nature, having escaped the corruption that is in the world by lust" (2 Pet 1:4). The nature of God is holiness, unalloyed with anything else. Thus, the writer of the book of Hebrews tells us that God chastises us to make us partakers of His holiness (Heb 12:10). Peter tells how our relationship with God should be changed when we have come to Christ: "But like the Holy One who called you, be holy yourselves also in all your behavior" (1 Pet 1:15). Peter then explains why, referring to what God said in Leviticus: "Because it is written, 'You shall be holy, for I am holy'" (v 16). In Leviticus 20, God describes to His people the punishment of sin and then prescribes what they should do: "You shall consecrate yourselves therefore and be holy, for I am the LORD your God. You shall keep My statutes and practice them; I am the LORD who sanctifies you...Thus you are to be holy to Me, for I the LORD am holy; and I have set you apart from the peoples to be Mine" (Lev 20:7–8, 26). Notice that God says we must consecrate, or sanctify, ourselves. If we do, He will sanctify us because He has separated us to be exclusively His. Because God is holy, we should perfect holiness in the fear of God.

Second, the Bible prescribes that holiness should characterize the human heart. Before anything changes in a person's life, the heart (the Bible's symbol for the center of the human will) must change first. The first thing that God says is, "Give me your heart." Then He says, "Watch your heart, for out of it come all the expressions of life" (see Prov 4:23). So the experience of holiness aims at changing the heart. When the heart is changed, then our attitude will change, our conversation will change, our thinking will change, and our actions will change. Did not Jesus say, "For the mouth speaks out of that which fills the heart" (Matt 12:34)? Did He not also say, "The good man brings out of his good treasure what is good; and the evil man brings out of his evil treasure what is evil" (Matt 12:35)? The Lord declares His aim to reclaim and restore His people by changing their hearts: "Then I will sprinkle clean water on you, and you will be clean; I will cleanse you from all your filthiness and from all your idols. Moreover, I will give you a new heart and put a new spirit within you; and I will remove the heart of stone from your flesh and give you a heart of flesh" (Ezek 36:25–26).

God urges His people to participate in the process of restoration, saying through His prophet, "Cast away from you all your transgressions which you have committed and make yourselves a new heart and a new spirit! For why will you die, O house of Israel?" (Ezek 18:31). Jesus put the emphasis on the purity or holiness of the heart, teaching us, "Blessed are the pure of heart, for they shall see God" (Matt 5:8). Sanctification or holiness begins when the Holy Spirit is in control of our heart. When the apostle Peter described the work of the Holy Spirit in the house of Cornelius to the council in Jerusalem, he said that the Spirit was "cleansing their hearts by faith" (Acts 15:8–9). The law of God is engraved upon our heart (i.e., our will) by the Spirit of God when complete cleansing takes place (Heb 10:16, 22). Only then, with a pure heart, can we truly love others (see 1 Tim 1:5; 1 Pet 1:22).

Third, the Word of God prescribes that holiness is the hallmark of the gift of the Holy Spirit in the life of the believer. The overall teaching of the Bible is that a believer receives the baptism or the infilling of the Holy Spirit sometime subsequent to conversion. Jesus said that the Holy Spirit is given to all those who ask for Him. His work is to guide, teach, remind, lead, purge, and empower the individual believer and the whole church. The Holy Spirit lives within our hearts. This is why He is called "the Spirit of holiness" (Rom 1:4), and we must be "sanctified by the Holy Spirit" (Rom 15:16). The law of the Holy Spirit in our heart gives us freedom from the law of sin (Rom 8:2). Writing to the Thessalonians, Paul says, "But we should always give thanks to God for you, brethren beloved by the Lord, because God has chosen you from the beginning for salvation through sanctification by the Spirit and faith in the truth" (2 Thess 2:13). The admonition of the Word is to "be filled with the Spirit" (Eph 5:18); because without Him there is no sanctification of the heart, no holiness of life, and no fruitfulness. Without Him, we cannot have true spiritual liberty (2 Cor 3:17).

Fourth, the Word of God prescribes holiness as characteristic of the believer's body. In other words, our body is set apart by the Spirit of God and is sanctified by Him. Our thoughts, desires, motives, and disposition can all be sanctified by the Spirit of God. The apostle Paul expresses such a need to the Thessalonians when he says, "Now may the God of peace Himself sanctify you entirely; and may your spirit and soul and body be preserved complete, without blame, at the coming of our Lord Jesus Christ" (1 Thess 5:23). Then he proceeds to tell them, "For this is the will of God, your sanctification; that is, that you abstain from sexual immorality; that each of you know how to possess his own vessel in sanctification and honor... For God has not called us for the purpose of impurity, but in sanctification" (1 Thess 4:3–4, 7). He further tells us that the body is the temple of God because the Spirit of God dwells in us: "Do you not know that you are a temple of God and that the Spirit of God dwells in you? If any man destroys the temple of God, God will destroy him" (1 Cor 3:16–17). Paul also reiterates this to the Ephesians when he says, "You also are being built together into a dwelling of God in the Spirit" (Eph 2:22).

Some phrases in the sixth chapter of Romans remind us that the prescription of holiness includes this mortal body of ours: "we have been buried with [Christ]"; "walk in newness of life"; "our old self was crucified with Him, in order that our body of sin might be done away with"; "so that we would no longer be slaves to sin"; "consider yourselves to be dead to sin"; "sin shall not be master over you"; "having been freed from sin, you became slaves of righteousness"; "present your members as slaves to righteousness, resulting in sanctification"; and "having been freed from sin and enslaved to God, you derive your benefit, resulting in sanctification, and the outcome, eternal life." The prescription for holiness in the Bible continues to be centered in our relationship with the brethren, the church, and in our relationship to the world, because holiness is relational in nature. It transforms all of our relationships: with God, with the church, with ourselves and with the world.

The Practice of Holiness

Holiness is a practical experience with tangible results, and it affects the totality of our life. However, the truth about holiness may be the most neglected doctrine in the church today. Its absence chastises us. Most of our troubles in the church can be traced to the absence of holiness. Lack of spiritual power and effectiveness in Christian mission and ministry are the direct results of the absence of holiness. Individualism and self-centeredness reign both in the pulpit and the pew. Disunity and conflict in the body of Christ have become like sour grapes in the teeth of those who observe the community of faith with dismay and disbelief. Believers' love has grown cold and commitment shallow due to the absence of personal holiness in the body of Christ. The absence of holiness has allowed secular culture to transform the church instead of the church's transforming culture. Holiness is the best source of power and authority for the people of God, as well as the best proof of the power and effectiveness of the gospel.

We have had a small glimpse of the need of the human heart for holiness. We have seen that believers' perceptions and approaches to a life of holiness vary, but that the prescription of the Bible for holiness is unmistakably clear. We are now ready to focus on the practice of holiness. How is holiness effected in our lives? What are the practical results of such an experience, and how does it manifest itself in our life?

The message of holiness has at times been obscured by fictitious claims, inconsistent lives, and a failure to sincerely examine the Scriptures. All of us stand in need of a revival of biblical holiness. Outside of the experience of holiness, the Church of God will be misdirected and confused in its mission and life. Christ said, "I came that they may have life, and have it abundantly" (John 10:10). What does such a life look like?

It is interesting to see how the holy life is described from different Christian perspectives. These perspectives help us discern the true practice of holiness compared to some of the counterfeits that have arisen in recent years.

Roger Green says, "Allowing for various definitions of holiness that are rooted in the biblical text, I continue to find strength in a definition of holiness as a life of obedience, rooted in love, to the Great Commandment of our Lord—to love God and love our neighbor supremely. In his work titled *The Way of Holiness*, Brengle wrote that, "'Sanctification is to have our sinful tempers cleansed, and our heart filled with love to God and man.'"[4]

Craig Keen says, "'Holiness' means, in the first place, what is peculiar to God. It is God's separateness, difference, from the world. Insofar as it is a true otherness. It is to be understood as God's qualitative distinction from all that God is not."[5]

---

4. Roger Green, "What Is Holiness?", in *The Holiness Manifesto*, ed. Kevin W. Mannoia and Don Thorsen, 233–34 (Grand Rapids, MI: William B. Eerdmans, 2008).

5. Craig Keen, "A Quick 'Definition' of Holiness," in *The Holiness Manifesto*, ed. Kevin W. Mannoia and Don Thorsen, 237–38 (Grand Rapids, MI: William B. Eerdmans, 2008).

Don Thorsen says, "Just as God is holy, God calls people to be holy. According to Scripture, God graciously makes holiness possible for people through the atonement of Jesus Christ our Savior. God further makes holiness possible through the presence and work of the Holy Spirit in the life of Christians, individually and collectively. God wants Christians to become entirely sanctified so as to reflect the likeness of Christ... Holiness encapsulates the sum of who God is and of how God wants Christians to think, speak and act in the world."[6]

Lisa R. Dorsey says, "God's people are to reflect a lifestyle that is distinctively different than that of the world. Although perfection, in the sense of God's perfection, is not obtained until Christ's return, there is a level of perfection that is obtainable to those who have been sanctified by the work of Christ on the cross and who are receiving the fullness of God's Spirit for this church era.... Hence, holiness is an outward manifestation of the inward work of Christ in the believer for His sovereign purposes."[7]

The Holiness Manifesto states, "God continues to work, giving life, hope, and salvation through the indwelling of the Holy Spirit, drawing us into God's own holy, loving life. God transforms us, delivering us from sin, idolatry, bondage, and self-centeredness to love and serve God, others, and to be stewards of creation. Thus, we are renewed in the image of God as revealed in Jesus Christ."[8]

In "Holiness for the 21st Century," it is argued that "the essence of holiness is Christ-likeness. It is the culture of God's Kingdom, engaging all the cultures of the world and powerful in drawing all people and nations to God. Holiness is both

6. Don Thorsen, "Holiness in the 21st Century," paper presented at the Holiness Association, [2005], 1.

7. Lisa R. Dorsey, "Holiness as Praxis," in *The Holiness Manifesto*, ed. Kevin W. Mannoia and Don Thorsen, 235–36 (Grand Rapids, MI: William B. Eerdmans, 2008).

8. Wesleyan Holiness Study Project, "The Holiness Manifestor," in *The Holiness Manifesto*, ed. Kevin W. Mannoia and Don Thorsen, 18–21 (Grand Rapids, MI: William B. Eerdmans, 2008).

a gift and a response, personal and communal, ethical and missional, requiring reflection and action."[9]

Russell R. Byrum writes, "By holiness of life is meant a life free from sin. It is a supernatural work of salvation and regeneration that makes holiness of life possible."[10]

So what is a workable definition of holiness? A comprehensive one is given by Dr. Orval J. Neace[11]:

1. *Holiness is cleansing.* It is the will of the Father, the provision of the Son, the act of the Holy Spirit, wherein the believer's heart—his motives, his affections, his will, his entire nature—is cleansed from the pollution and the tendency to sin.

2. *Holiness is harmony.* Complete inner harmony is not realized in regeneration. The Bible and experience agree that the unsanctified heart is a divided heart, a double heart. Outward defeat is occasioned by inward disharmony. Sanctification rids the soul of the inner foe and aligns the forces of the moral nature against the outer enemy.

3. *Holiness is abandonment.* The church fathers referred to the act of human cooperation in sanctification as crucifixion of self, a deathbed consecration. They meant a giving over of the all of one's life to the plan and authority of God. The man who is sanctified is thus given over to God.

4. *Holiness is power.* Power is in the spiritual realm, the realm immediately affected by sanctification. Sanctification affects all that one is. Such endowment of power—the ability to discriminate, to evaluate, to

---

9. A working document of the Wesleyan Holiness Project, Azusa, CA (May 3, 2005).

10. Russell R. Byrum, *Christian Theology* (Anderson, IN: Warner Press, 1925), 440.

11. Quoted in H. Orton Wiley, *Christian Theology*, vol 3 (Kansas City, MO: Beacon Hill Press, 1943) 8.

command one's will—can be realized as power from on high possesses the believer.

5. *Holiness is perfection in love.* The sanctified one is not beyond the ability, nor liability to sin, but he is cleansed from the desire and nature of sin. He is not beyond the possibility of fall, but within the provision of divine grace he is preserved from willful transgression.

Sanctification is not fixedness of character but fixedness of attitude and desire, enabling the recipient to grow in grace and in the knowledge of our Lord and Savior Jesus Christ.

It is helpful to review Wesley's eleven points from *A Plain Account of Christian Perfection* in which he outlines what Christian perfection is and what it is not:

1. There is such a thing as perfection, for it is again and again mentioned in the Scriptures.

2. It is not as early as justification; for justified persons are to "go on to perfection" (Heb 6:1 NKJV).

3. It is not as late as death, for St. Paul speaks of living persons that were perfect (Phil 3:15).

4. It is not absolute. Absolute perfection belongs not to humans, nor to angels, but to God alone.

5. It does not make a person infallible. No one is infallible while he or she remains in the body.

6. Is it sinless? It is not worthwhile to contend for a term. It is salvation from sin.

7. It is perfect love (1 John 4:18). This is the essence of it: its properties are inseparable fruits, rejoicing always, praying without ceasing, and in everything giving thanks (1 Thess 5:16).

8. It is improvable. It is so far from lying in an individual point, from being incapable to increase, that those

perfected in love may grow in grace far swifter than they did before.

9. It is amissible, that is, it is capable of being lost.

10. It is constantly both preceded and followed by a gradual work.

11. It is instantaneous in that there must be an actual moment where self dies and sin ceases, even though some may not perceive the instant.[12]

God wants all of His people to enter into an intimate relationship with Him through the experience of holiness. Our model is Christ, our authority the Word of God, and our boast the presence and the power of the Holy Spirit. Just because some have failed in the experience, some have misrepresented the experience, and some have gone to the extremes of being legalistic without expressing much genuine love, this does not invalidate the will of God for His people. Failures on the way of holiness do not disprove the urgent need for holiness and the undeniable promise of Scripture.

The Power of Holiness

The direct influence of the Holy Spirit upon a person's life is a clear testimony to the power of God. Paul says, "The law of the Spirit of life in Christ Jesus has set you free from the law of sin and of death" (Rom 8:2). The Bible and personal experience testify to the fact that the experience of holiness provides spiritual authority, courage, boldness, and power in the life of the believer.

First, the Holy Spirit gives power to Christian worship. On the day of Pentecost, when the Holy Spirit came upon them, the disciples found not only purity of heart but also a divine

---

12. As paraphrased by Doug Cullum. "Holiness of Heart and Life: Wesley's Vision of Christian Existence," paper. http://www.holinessandunity.org/index. php?option=com_docman&task=doc_download&gid=17&Itemid=

power that delivered them from the fear of people. Therefore, they could boldly stand and testify of the resurrection of Christ. In Acts 4, we read that after being threatened by the civil authorities, the disciples found refuge in the fellowship of the church and engaged in fervent prayer. The Bible says that after they had prayed, the place where they had gathered together was shaken and they were all filled with the Holy Spirit and began to speak the word of God with boldness" (Acts 4:31).

The fullness of the Holy Spirit releases us from self-centeredness and timidity to worship God in Spirit and truth. The Spirit causes us to be overtaken with the awe, reverence, and fear of God. I believe many congregations have lost the essence of worship today because they have made it all a matter of aesthetics, concerned about what makes us feel good. Holiness focuses on the majesty of God, causing us to yield to His supremacy and be filled with holy fear, reverence, and awe. Could it be that Christian worship is so shallow today because the lack of holiness has robbed us of the fear and reverence of God? Who can see or hear God without being filled with reverence and bowing down to cry, "Holy, holy, holy is the Lord"?

Second, the Holy Spirit gives power to unify the body of Christ. Theoretically, most of us believe that there is one body, one faith, and one Lord. But practically, we are divided by creed, by race, by ethnicity, by social status, by aesthetics, and by personal likes and dislikes. It is not by accident that the apostle Paul says that the Spirit gives life and then admonishes us to "keep the unity of the Spirit" (Eph 4:3). Holiness unites us with all those in whom the Spirit bears witness that they are the children of God.

David W. Kendall says, "Earnest believers will seek to counter the radical individualism of Western Culture. Such individualism caters to human self-centeredness, fosters self-reliance, and thus encourages independence from God and isolation from one another. In contrast God calls us to be a people, a family whose love for Him unites us in passionate pursuit of Christ-likeness."[13] You see, the power of the Holy Spirit removes the barriers that keep us apart, and when the love of God is shed abroad in our hearts by the Holy Spirit, he draws us to each other. Christian disunity testifies to the absence of true holiness and love. Notice what the scripture says: "And the congregation of those who believed were of one heart and soul" (Acts 4:32). All of the tensions and struggles within the body of Christ could be healed by the power of holiness, because holiness changes our hearts and alters our behavior.

Third, the Holy Spirit gives us power to resist temptation. Holiness does not free us from temptation, just as it does not free us from the ability to sin. But the power of temptation lies in the desire of the heart and the lust of the flesh. Since holiness delivers us from the desire and the will to sin, then our temptation is not from within but from without. The Bible instructs us as to the attitude that we should have toward temptation and its outcome: "no temptation has overtaken you but such as is common to man; and God is faithful, who will not allow you to be tempted beyond what you are able, but with the temptation will provide the way of escape also, so that you will be able to endure it" (1 Cor 10:13).

Fourth, the Holy Spirit exercises power over our disposition and affects our attitude toward the circumstances of life. A Spirit-filled believer has a disposition of kindness, joy, and hope, and is free of competitiveness and negative expressions. This is why Scripture says, "Finally, brethren, whatever is true, whatever is honorable, whatever is right, whatever is pure, whatever is lovely, whatever is of good repute, if there is any excellence and if anything worthy of praise, dwell on these things" (Phil 4:8).

---

13. David W. Kendall, "The Holiness to Which We Are Called," paper. http://holinessandunity.org/index.php?option=com_docman&task=doc_download&gid=22&Itemid=

Fifth, the Holy Spirit liberates and empowers us for witness and effective service. Since the experience of holiness has freed us from the inner disunity and disharmony, we can be motivated by the divine love that has been shed abroad in our hearts by the Holy Spirit (Rom 5:5). Holiness is both redemptive and missional in nature, so a human heart guided by the Holy Spirit illuminates the world with the message of love and truth. Holiness constitutes both authority and passion in our life for witness. Notice what the book of Acts says about the disciples after that great encounter with the Holy Spirit on the Day of Pentecost: "And with great power the apostles were giving testimony to the resurrection of the Lord Jesus, and abundant grace was upon them all" (Acts 4:33). That power works in us, moving us, equipping us, and enabling us to communicate the love of God for the redemption of the world (see Eph 3:20).

II.

Current Questions about the

HOLY SPIRIT

———

7. A Closer Look at the Gift of Tongues

The Christian community has disagreements about various aspects of the Holy Spirit's work, but none is so intense or divisive as the one over the gift of tongues. It is not our intent here to add to the confusion, nor to do a full exposition on the gift of speaking in tongues; but rather to lift some biblical insights that will help us focus on the essential truths about spiritual gifts.

We have seen clearly from the Word of God that the gift of the Holy Spirit has been promised to all believers, but in making that promise Jesus did not say anything about the gifts of the Spirit. He said, "You will receive power" (Acts 1:8); "He abides with you and will be in you" (John 14:17); "He will guide you into all the truth" (John 16:13); "He will teach you all things, and bring to your remembrance all that I said to you" (John 14:26). However, the gospel accounts tell us nothing about the gifts of the Spirit. Jesus' silence about spiritual gifts seems to imply that he emphasized our need to receive the Holy Spirit himself. We can manifest all sorts of ministry gifts, but if we do not have the divine giver, they will avail us nothing.

The book of Acts records that the gift of tongues followed the outpouring of the Holy Spirit on three occasions. It should be noted that nowhere in these accounts or elsewhere in the New Testament is the phrase "unknown tongues" used. The translators of the King James Version used this expression to signify that they were unsure of the meaning of the original

79

Greek. This is why the King James Version italicizes the word *unknown* in the phrase; it is a word supplied by the translators, not a translation of the Greek text itself. The words used in the Greek New Testament are *eterais glossais*, "other languages." Even in modern Greek translations of the New Testament, the words are *eterais glossais*, which also mean "other languages."

The first occasion of this gift was on the day of Pentecost, as it is recorded in Acts 2:1–8. The Holy Spirit came and rested upon each of the disciples as if tongues of fire rested upon them, and they spoke in *eterais glossais*, "other languages." Their audience was primarily Jewish, including those who had come in from the Diaspora for the celebration of the Pentecost feast, so they spoke in various dialects. Yet Scripture says that all of them heard the disciples speak in their own language.

The second occasion occurred when Peter visited the house of Cornelius (Acts 10:44–47). As Peter preached the word to Cornelius and his Gentile household, there was an outpouring of the Spirit and they began speaking in "various languages" (*lalounton glossais*). The Jews who had come with Peter witnessed the outpouring of the Spirit upon the Gentiles in the same way that He came upon the Jewish disciples on the day of Pentecost. Yet these converts were all Gentiles, the other sheep that Jesus was calling into the fold.

The third occasion recorded by the book of Acts occurred when Paul visited certain believers at Ephesus (Acts 19:1–6). Scripture tells us that Paul shared Christ with them and baptized them in the name of the Lord Jesus, "And when Paul had laid his hands upon them, the Holy Spirit came on them, and they began speaking with tongues [*elallou te glossais*, literally "spoke in languages"], and prophesying."

These are the only three instances in the New Testament in which people received the Holy Spirit and spoke in tongues. Notice that, in each case, a *group* of believers was involved; Scripture never describes an individual who received the Holy Spirit in private and then spoke in tongues. For example, Paul received the Holy Spirit by the laying on of hands by Ananias, but he did not speak in tongues. On the other hand, the Bible describes some groups on whom there was an outpouring of the Holy Spirit but they did not speak in tongues. When Philip preached in Samaria, there was a great revival, the apostles laid their hands on the converts, and they received the Holy Spirit, but no one spoke in tongues. Acts 4:31 describes a large assembly of believers who prayed, the place was shaken, and all of them were filled with the Holy Spirit, but no one spoke in tongues.

How do we account for these differences? It appears that the gift of speaking in tongues is a sign to unbelievers. The Holy Spirit gave some believers this ability whenever and wherever the need presented itself. We believe that they were speaking in known human languages because in each of the instances recorded in Acts, there was no need for interpretation. The audience understood what the Spirit-filled believers were saying, without an interpreter.

These references to the gift of tongues in the book of Acts lead us to the following conclusions:

a. There is a divine gift that can enable someone to speak in other tongues or languages without previously having learned them.

b. This gift of tongues does not need interpretation.

c. This divine gift of speaking in other tongues may be received when one receives the Holy Spirit, but it is not always received with the Holy Spirit.

d. The genuine gift of speaking in tongues is used to address other human beings, not God. We do not need another language to speak to God; He understands whatever language we already know.

e. Each time the genuine gift of tongues was manifested in the book of Acts, it signified the universality of the gospel message. It demonstrated that God is not a respecter of persons, but "whoever will call on the name of the Lord will be saved" (Rom 10:13).

f. In none of these instances did the gift call attention to the presence of the Holy Spirit. The Holy Spirit's intent, even when he endowed believers with the gift of tongues, was to exalt Christ and not himself.

We owe a great deal to the apostle Paul for categorizing and explaining the spiritual gifts. Paul had to deal extensively with the gifts due to their misuse, abuse, and even counterfeiting in the church of Corinth.

Much of the modern controversy concerning the gift of speaking in tongues arises from Paul's treatment of the subject in 1 Corinthians 14. Although he also refers to this gift in Romans 12 and 1 Corinthians 12, we are confronted with a real challenge when we come to the fourteenth chapter of 1 Corinthians. Does this chapter have to do with the genuine gift? Is Paul dealing with a counterfeit spiritual manifestation that had arisen in Corinth? Or is he talking about the edifying use of multiple languages that are usually found in a cosmopolitan congregation? Answers do not come easy.

The church of Corinth was a multinational, multicultural, and multilingual church. It was located in a cosmopolitan city where all the vices of idolatry and wickedness reigned without restraint. Those who were converted into the Christian faith had the tendency to bring along some of their old practices in their newfound faith. That had caused both concern and confusion in the church.

Paul rebukes the Corinthian church as being carnal, divisive, in a state of confusion, and practicing some gross sins that were worse than those among the Gentiles. He calls the members of the church "babes in Christ" who are not in a position to deal with serious spiritual matters. Immaturity seems to be the norm in the Corinthian church. Thus, the people fell prey to the abuse, misuse, counterfeits, and confusion with respect to the spiritual gifts, in particular the gift of speaking in tongues. (Remember that nowhere in the original Greek text of this chapter is the expression for "unknown tongues" used.)

What is the apostle Paul trying to correct in the church of Corinth? What is being practiced here that causes such confusion with respect to spiritual gifts? Let's state several possibilities that have been suggested. Then, by using the process of elimination, we will try to identify the problem with which the apostle Paul is dealing.

a. *A language of the soul.* Some Bible commentators believe Paul refers to an unuttered expression of worship characteristic of a believer who has a burden of the soul that can be expressed only in groans: "In the same way the Spirit also helps our weakness; for we do not know how to pray as we should, but the Spirit Himself intercedes for us with groanings too deep for words" (Rom 8:26). "We groan, longing to be clothed with our dwelling from heaven...Now He who prepared us for this very purpose is God, who gave to us the Spirit as a pledge" (2 Cor 5:2, 5). However, if this were the case, why would the apostle Paul try to correct or regulate it in 1 Corinthians 14?

b. *The supernatural ability to speak another human language.* In other words, some believe that 1 Corinthians 14 refers to another manifestation of the Pentecostal gift. However, it is significant that in this chapter Paul does not mention "the Spirit" or "the Holy Spirit." He states in verse 12 that the Corinthians are "zealous of spirits" (*zelotai este pneumaton*), not "spiritual gifts" as the King James Version translates it. If Paul intended to say that the Corinthians were "zealous of spiritual gifts," the text should have said *zelotai este pneumatikon*. The meaning of this verse is crucial to our understanding. Also notice that Paul calls for interpretation of this utterance, so it

83

is doubtful that he is dealing with the gift of speaking in languages that a diverse audience would understand. As we noted earlier, that gift did not need interpretation.

c. *An unintelligible language.* Some scholars believe that Paul was condemning a Christian manifestation of something practiced by the worshipers of the goddess Aphrodite. During their worship, those people came under some ecstatic spell and began babbling unintelligible sounds, which they claimed was proof that they were possessed by the goddess they worshiped. Was such a practice transferred (intentionally or unintentionally) into the early church? Were the Coinrthians trying to yield themselves to the influence of some kind of alien "spirits," as in verse 12? We do not know! Unintelligible babbling sounds would have suggested such an influence, and there might have been some of this among new believers who lived in a pagan city. But we find no conclusive evidence to support this theory. Why would Paul call for someone to interpret what no human being could understand? Yet Paul calls for interpretation of these utterances.

d. *The natural language of each individual.* As the city of Corinth was a cosmopolitan center with various nationalities and languages, so was the church. It seems likely that several foreign languages were spoken in the church. If so, passionate believers might stand up in a worship service and try to speak in their own native language, even though it was not understood by many of the others. Since this chapter says nothing about an "unknown tongue," and since the genuine gift of tongues does not need interpretation, Paul must have been referring to a human language which could be understood and interpreted. Yet that was not happening. When the Corinthians spoke in their "tongues," the result was confusion. It is foolish to speak to people in a language they do not understand. Even though the speaker understands, the hearer does not, and Paul says that does not edify the church. Therefore, the speaker in "another tongue" needs an interpreter or it is better to remain quiet in public. Could it be that the confusion over tongues in the church of Corinth was caused by the improper use of the natural languages of those congregating in the church? The multicultural context of the church in Corinth points in this direction.

As we saw in the book of Acts, the genuine Holy Spirit gift of tongues is given in the time of need so that the message of the gospel can be communicated to a diverse audience without an interpreter. This gift does not cause confusion. It does not divide the people of God. It makes unbelievers stand in awe of what God is able to do. And it edifies the church by leading believers into a harmonious fellowship (*koinonia*).

Paul tells the Corinthian Christians that genuine spiritual gifts do not compete with each other. Rather, they complement one another for the benefit of the church. He says that the genuine gift of tongues is not the evidence that one has received the Holy Spirit. Further, Paul says that we should not seek the gift of tongues, because the Holy Spirit confers his gifts whenever he wills, upon whomsoever he wills. So Paul admonishes the Corinthians (and us!) to seek the giver and not his gifts.

8. The "Manifestations" of the Spirit

The Bible is like a treasure chest, describing the great variety of the Holy Spirit's manifestations in the world, in the church, and in the life of the individual believer. No other theme is so intricately interwoven from the first chapter of Genesis to the last chapter of Revelation. The Spirit may be variously identified as the Holy Spirit; the Spirit of Wisdom; the Spirit of Christ; the Spirit of Revelation; and the Spirit of Fire.

The Bible says, "And the Spirit of God was moving over the surface of the waters" (Gen 1:2). Again it says, "For the letter kills, but the Spirit gives life" (2 Cor 3:6). It was, therefore, the Holy Spirit who breathed into the nostrils of man and he became a living soul, for the Spirit is the breath of God. Thus God says, "'Not by might nor by power, but by My Spirit,' says the LORD of hosts" (Zech 4:6). It is not an accident that the human heart always prays, "And do not take Your Holy Spirit from me" (Ps 51:11). And the hymn writer expresses the longing of every believer when he says, "With Thy Spirit fill me; Make me wholly Thine, I pray."[1]

Yet, conflict and the confusion over the Holy Spirit are greater today than they were at the church of Corinth. So many bizarre things are attributed to the Holy Spirit that some of them border blasphemy. There is a real danger that, in our thirst for the Spirit's fullness, we may attribute things to Him

---

1. "With Thy Spirit Fill Me." Words by B. D. Ackley. Copyright © 1940. © Renewed 1968 by The Rodeheaver Company.

that are contrary to His nature. We said earlier that the church held many councils in the early centuries to try to clarify its understanding of the Holy Spirit. The irony of our day is that our hottest debates are not about the Holy Spirit but about His manifestations. So many Christians seek His manifestations rather than seeking Him.

A manifestation of the Holy Spirit is known through the physical senses rather than through the special revelation of God's Word. Therein lies the danger: Our senses can easily be deceived. Further, there is a tendency to confuse manifestations of the Spirit with the gifts of the Spirit. Even though there is a relationship between the two, there is a distinct difference.

In our days, contradictory claims about four manifestations of the Spirit have caused great division and confusion within the body of Christ. These manifestations are touted as definitive evidence of the Holy Spirit and His work. Two of these manifestations are being slain in the Spirit and holy laughter. Worshipers are said to be slain in the Spirit when someone touches them on the forehead and they fall into a swoon. There is no biblical foundation for this practice and no record in the New Testament that the Holy Spirit ever manifested himself in this way. Holy laughter—uncontrollable, frenetic laughter during a worship service—also has no biblical foundation. Nowhere in the New Testament is holy laughter noted as being an activity of the Holy Spirit.

We explained earlier that speaking in an unknown tongue or a prayer language has no scriptural validity as a manifestation of the Holy Spirit; however, the Spirit does occasionally enable believers to speak in other languages. This biblical gift of tongues (i.e., the supernatural ability to speak in other human languages) may have two purposes according to the New Testament. In some instances (e.g., the Day of Pentecost), it is the means that God uses to communicate His Word when there is no other means. In other instances, this sudden ability to speak in other languages serves as a sign to unbelievers.

But nowhere does the New Testament state or imply that this genuine gift of speaking in tongues is definitive evidence that one has the Holy Spirit.

God is not the author of confusion or division, but the promotion of these so-called manifestations of the Spirit causes both confusion and division in the body of Christ. True manifestations of the Holy Spirit contribute to the unity of the body and the spreading of the gospel. It will be helpful if we review these.

The New Testament indicates that the first visible manifestation of the Spirit is conviction. Jesus said, "And He, when He comes, will convict the world concerning sin and righteousness and judgment" (John 16:8). The Holy Spirit reveals, convicts, and rebukes our sin. This is why on the day of Pentecost the listeners "were pierced to the heart, and said to Peter and the rest of the apostles, 'Brethren, what shall we do?'" (Acts 2:37).

A second visible manifestation of the Spirit is the unity of believers. He breaks down the barriers that divide people. He baptizes with fire and love. He changes human nature so that even enemies are drawn to each other. Thus it was said about the believers after the Pentecost that "all those who had believed were together" (Acts 2:44). "And the congregation of those who believed were of one heart and soul" (Acts 2:32). Wherever the Holy Spirit is at work, people are united and live harmoniously for the cause of Christ. The Spirit draws people who believe to Christ and to each other.

Praise is another obvious manifestation of the Spirit. It is the Spirit's purpose to exalt and lift up Christ. Since the Holy Spirit puts joy in our heart (for joy is the fruit of the Spirit), He fills our lips with praise. Jesus makes it clear that the Holy Spirit will speak of Him and that He will glorify Him (John 16:14). There is no dull worship, listless singing, or apathetic living when the Holy Spirit is at work among God's people. His praise fills their lips with psalms and spiritual songs.

The New Testament suggests that another manifestation of the Holy Spirit's presence is prayer. Not only does the Spirit teach us to pray, but he also helps us to pray and makes intercession on our behalf. "In the same way the Spirit also helps our weakness; for we do not know how to pray as we should, but the Spirit Himself intercedes for us with groanings too deep for words; and He who searches the hearts knows what the mind of the Spirit is, because He intercedes for the saints according to the will of God" (Rom 8:26–27). Any outpouring of genuine prayer is influenced by the Spirit, and He makes our daily discipline of prayer to come alive.

Another manifestation of the Spirit is believers' holiness of life. The Spirit is our purifier and sanctifier. The absence of personal holiness will obscure other manifestations of the Spirit. Holiness is the nature of the Spirit, and whoever lives in the Spirit manifests a life of holiness. It is unrealistic to expect other manifestations of the Spirit where personal holiness is absent. The Spirit helps us to be partakers of Christ's holiness (Heb 12:10) and enables us to perfect holiness in the fear of God (2 Cor 7:1). And He produces in us the fruit of holiness to the extent that we yield ourselves to become servants of holiness. You may not have many notable gifts when the Holy Spirit possesses your life, but you cannot be possessed by Him and remain unholy.

The outward manifestations of the Spirit are several, but I would like to mention one more. This is the manifestation of spiritual power, which becomes evident in two ways:

1. A believer can stand courageously to do the will of God and fulfill His purpose.
2. A believer can exercise authority over the Enemy of our souls.

The powers of darkness are made subject to the authority of the Spirit, and His power enables us to be effective in the ministry of the gospel. To that effect, the Lord Jesus Christ promised his disciples, "You will receive power when the Holy Spirit has come upon you; and you shall be My witnesses both in Jerusalem, and in all Judea and Samaria, and even to the remotest part of the earth" (Acts 1:8).

As we noted above with respect to the gifts of the Spirit, the manifestations of the Spirit are essential, but not as essential as the Holy Spirit himself. Too often we get so enamored with the gifts and manifestations that we forget the giver. The Spirit has come to deal with our needs, to be our helper, and to help us in our struggles. He is able to help us in our weaknesses, teach us, guide us, empower us, and sanctify us so that we can effectively serve His Church and confront the world with the good news of the gospel.

Have you experienced the Holy Spirit? Life's victory comes "'not by might nor by power, but by My Spirit,' says the Lord of hosts" (Zech 4:6). No doubt such a genuine experience is needed in the church today.

9. The Healing Ministry of the Holy Spirit

Another area of confusion and disagreement about the Holy Spirit's ministry concerns healing. Many believers expect miraculous acts of physical healing to demonstrate the Holy Spirit's presence among them. Like so many other things, this belief is rooted in the truth, but it has been distorted to suit the selfish purposes of religious hucksters. To understand what the Bible teaches about the Spirit's healing work, we need to focus on the symbol of fire.

The prophet Malachi foretold that when the Messiah came, he would be "like a refiner's fire…a refiner and purifier of silver" (Mal 3:2, 3). Jesus confirmed this by saying, "I have come to cast fire upon the earth" (Luke 12:49).

Fire can be destructive, as with the fire and brimstone that came upon the cities of Sodom and Gomorrah. But fire can also purify, refine, and heal. It is in this sense that the Bible often represents the Holy Spirit's ministry as one of fire.

John the Baptist said of Jesus, "He will baptize you with the Holy Spirit and fire" (Matt 3:11). On the day of Pentecost, The Holy Spirit came upon them, appearing as "tongues as of fire" (Acts 2:3). The fire of the Holy Spirit burns away all that is unnecessary, consumes all that defiles, and heals all that decays. Thus, the prophet said that the Holy Spirit is like the fire that a jeweler uses to purifies silver and gold. He removes all that defiles the soul in order to present it to God holy, without spot or blemish.

It is one thing to know Christ as our Savior, but it quite another to know Him as our refiner. It is one thing to know Christ as our Lord, but it is quite another to know Him as our sanctifier in the power of the Holy Spirit. What we need today is a fresh touch of the fire of the Holy Spirit.

The fire of the Holy Spirit will awaken the church from the sleep of spiritual death. His fire will deliver us from backsliding. His fire will heal relationships in the church quicker than anything else. The fire of the Holy Spirit will heal the church of division and carnality, melting our hearts together. A fresh fire of the Holy Spirit will heal the church from the spirit of the world. Let's consider some of the ways in which the Spirit's fire can heal us:

First, the Holy Spirit heals us from the ugliness of sin. All of us have been infected by sin. This spiritual infection manifests itself in various ways in the life of the church and the individual believer. For example, is apparent in a mind that is confused, wicked, and selfish; in a heart that is deceptive and bitter; in a tongue that lies and gossips; in a perverted, pleasure-seeking will; in feelings of resentment and anger.

The apostle Paul cries in the seventh chapter of Romans, Who will remove from me all this evil within me? Then in the eighth chapter, he concludes this can only come about by the law of the spirit of God.

Second, the Holy Spirit heals our selfish motives. Many of us do a lot of good things with the wrong motives. We can preach, teach, sing, and give with the wrong motive. In fact, most conflicts and problems in the church arise when Christian people act out of the wrong motives. The motive could be recognition, self-gratification, or a host of other things.

See how selfish were the motives of Ananias and Sapphira (see Acts 5:1–16). They wanted to make a good impression in the community of the apostles. Every person was selling their possessions and bringing the money to the apostles for the advancement of the kingdom and the aid of their poor brethren.

In order to impress their friends, Ananias and Sapphira lied—not only to the apostles but to the Holy Spirit. We are tempted to do many things for selfish reasons, but the fresh fire of the Holy Spirit can heal us from selfishness.

Third, the Holy Spirit heals us from the sting of our self-centeredness. We see the mark of selfishness in all of us. It is not by accident that Jesus said anyone who wants to be His disciple must first deny himself (Matt 16:24). Wow! How do you do that? None of us can be productive in the kingdom without submitting ourselves fully to God and being healed by the fresh fire of the Holy Spirit. Jesus said, "Whoever wishes to save his life will love it; but whoever loses his life for My sake will find it" (Matt 16:25). The Spirit can enable us to do that.

Fourth, the fire of the Holy Spirit heals us from destructive emotions. Some people's feelings determine everything they do in life: feelings of loneliness, of depression, of anger, of envy, and so on. Modern society says, "Express what you feel. Don't hold your feelings in. Let them out." But are these feelings from God or from the self? Are they the result of sin? You will recall that one fruit of the Spirit is temperance or self-control. The Greek word is *egkrateia* ("to hold back," "to tell yourself no"). In other words, a Spirit-filled person does not always allow himself to do what he feels like doing. You and I are incapable of exercising full self-control, but the Holy Spirit can help us do that. The fresh fire of the Holy Spirit can heal us from the devastating effects of self-centered emotions.

Finally, the Holy Spirit heals us from divisiveness. The Bible speaks repeatedly about the unity of the Spirit. Divisiveness comes from sin and self-orientation, but the Bible says that if we live in the Spirit or if we walk in the Spirit, we shall not fulfill the works of the flesh. Then we will be able to live with other believers in the unity of the Spirit.

10. The Offense against the Holy Spirit

The best companion that God has given to guide, sustain, and equip us for life and ministry is the Holy Spirit. Christ promises us that the Holy Spirit not only will be with us, but in us. But we are warned: "Do not grieve the Holy Spirit of God, by whom you were sealed for the day of redemption" (Eph 4:30).

We need to remember that, because the Holy Spirit is a person, He can be offended, grieved, and alienated by our attitude, our behavior, our words, and our feelings. God says, "My Spirit shall not strive with men forever" (Gen 6:3). When our offense is persistent, the Holy Spirit can withdraw Himself from any individual or congregation. How can such an offense occur?

- We offend the Holy Spirit when we regard Him as a mere impersonal object. "The Spirit Himself testifies with our spirit that we are the children of God" (Rom 8:16).
- We offend the Holy Spirit when we regard Him as any person less than God.
- We offend the Holy Spirit when we attempt to achieve our spiritual goals without him.
- We offend the Holy Spirit when we depend more on gifts, talents, learning, or other things rather than on His presence and power to accomplish the work of God.

Stephen condemned his persecutors by saying, "You men who are stiff-necked and uncircumcised in heart and ears are always resisting the Holy Spirit; you are doing just as your fathers did" (Acts 7:51). The implication here is that we resist the Holy Spirit when we oppose those whom the Holy Spirit has anointed to do his work.

The Bible uses three different words to denote an offense against the Holy Spirit. Each one gives us a slightly different perspective on how this can occur. Isaiah 63:10 says that the people of Israel "rebelled and grieved His Holy Spirit; therefore He turned Himself to become their enemy, and He fought against them." We should note two words here. One is "grieved" (Hebrew *ruah*, which is close to the Greek *lupeo* in meaning). In its strictest sense, this word means that they had annoyed, provoked, or challenged the Spirit of God. The other word is "rebelled." They openly defied anything that the Spirit of God directed them to do. Thus, He became their enemy and fought against them. It is very dangerous to persist in resisting the Holy Spirit, who is God's messenger of reconciliation.

The second biblical word that describes an offense against the Holy Spirit appears when Paul says, "Do not quench the Spirit" (1 Thess 5:19). The Greek word for "quench" is *sbennumi*, from the root word *sbeno* (to snuff out, to extinguish). It essentially means to "put out" a light or fire. The word can also be used figuratively to mean "dampen, hinder, repress," as in preventing the Holy Spirit from exerting His full influence.

The Holy Spirit is quenched when we do some act, speak some word, or display some temper that is contrary to the Spirit:

- *He is the Spirit of love.* Therefore, anger and malice can cause Him to withdraw His influence.
- *He is the Spirit of peace.* Therefore, personal attacks and contentiousness that disrupt the unity of the body of Christ may quench Him.
- *He is the Spirit of joy.* Therefore, pessimistic, negative, skeptical talk may quench Him.

Whatever the cause, we know that the Holy Spirit has been quenched when His influence is withdrawn, His presence is not felt, His joy is not expressed, and His power is not manifested. It is imperative in our assemblies of deliberation and gatherings of worship that we be sensitive to the leadings of the Holy Spirit and follow His dictates in all that we do.

The third word that Scripture uses to describe an offense toward the Holy Spirit is a word used by Paul that is also translated as "grieving" the Spirit: "Do not grieve the Holy Spirit of God, by whom you were sealed for the day of redemption" (Eph 4:30). The Greek word here is *lupeite*, which means "to grieve, afflict with sorrow." The same word appears in Romans 14:15, where Paul cautions us not to grieve or offend a Christian brother by eating food that he considers to be unclean.

A most literal translation of the Ephesians 4 passage should be, "Do not cause God the Spirit to weep by the way you live or the way you behave." What might we do that would cause the Holy Spirit to weep? Paul names several specific things.

First, he mentions bitterness of spirit (Greek *pasa pikria*, literally "every bitterness"). This Greek word comes from *pikros*, which describes the bitterness of an herb or a fruit that sets your whole body on edge. Thus, when we allow circumstances or actions or words to sour us or make us bitter, we cause the Spirit of God to weep. The Holy Spirit cannot dwell or work in a bitter soul.

The second thing that Paul mentions is anger (Greek *thumos*). This word literally means "a violent motion or passion of the mind," which in the most cases involves the desire to inflict punishment on someone else. Anger is not compatible with the workings of the Holy Spirit. It cannot accomplish the will of God, and it grieves the Holy Spirit because it runs counter to His nature.

The third thing that the apostle Paul says will grieve the Holy Spirit is rage (Gk. *orge*, from *orego*, which means "to covet after or desire"). Rage is depicted as the outburst of a vengeful mind.

Aristotle said that *orge* is "desire with grief." Rage always expresses itself with vengeful acts and injurious words. The rage of man never works the will of God, and the rage of a believer not only grieves the Holy Sprit but totally interrupts His influence.

One more thing should be mentioned as grieving of the Spirit in the life of the believer and the church: clamor (Greek *krauge*, from *krazo*, "to thrash about or cry"). The word suggests any kind of tumult, controversy, or careless talk that grieves the Holy Spirit.

The Spirit of God is holy, gentle, and sensitive. Our attitudes, our words, and our behavior can offend Him, grieve Him, and quench His influence in our lives. We should keep in focus Paul's twofold command: "do not quench the Spirit" and "do not grieve the Spirit of God."

The teaching of Christ on this sober subject is recorded by three of the Evangelists as follows:

Therefore I say to you, any sin and blasphemy shall be forgiven people, but blasphemy against the Spirit shall not be forgiven. Whoever speaks a word against the Son of Man, it shall be forgiven him; but whoever speaks against the Holy Spirit, it shall not be forgiven him, either in this age or in the age to come. (Matt 12:31–32)

"Truly I say to you, all sins shall be forgiven the sons of men, and whatever blasphemies they utter; but whoever blasphemes against the Holy Spirit never has forgiveness, but is guilty of an eternal sin"—because they were saying, "He has an unclean spirit." (Mark 3:28–30)

And everyone who speaks a word against the Son of Man, it will be forgiven him; but he who blasphemes against the Holy Spirit, it will not be forgiven him. (Luke 12:10)

God's grace deals with all of us in a gentle way to bring us to the saving knowledge of Jesus Christ. And the Holy Spirit convicts us of sin and draws us to Christ, so that we might experience salvation. But there is such a thing as resistance to the Spirit of grace. It is a willful and determined opposition to the power of the Holy Spirit.

How do we know if we committed blasphemy against the Holy Spirit? When have we committed the "unpardonable sin"? Some people worry incessantly that they might have committed the sin against the Holy Spirit. The very fact that they are concerned may be the best indicator that they have not committed such a sin.

However, Scripture warns that some do always resist the Holy Ghost, people who in their self-complacency and pride trample under foot the Son of God. Those who sin against the Holy Spirit have no thought about their eternal destiny. They are deaf to the promptings of God. They harden themselves like steel against any attempt by God to lead them to repentance and reconciliation. They have a persistent rebellion against God, seasoned with indifference and insensibility.

This sin is unpardonable, not because God's grace is insufficient or because God is unwilling to grant them mercy but because they have despised and rejected the only agent of reconciliation, the Holy Spirit. This renders them incapable of repentance or faith.

In some people, this state is very visible; in others, it is not. There are not always clear outward signs by which we can discern that a person has committed the unpardonable sin. Some will be openly defiant against God, while others are oblivious to their sealed doom.

Some offenses against the Holy Spirit can be forgiven. One may grieve, quench, or even offend the Holy Spirit and still find mercy and forgiveness when he returns to the Lord with a repentant attitude. But this should not lull us into a sense of complacency. There is a sin against the Holy Spirit or a blasphemy against Him that will not be forgiven and that constitutes the "unpardonable sin."

Our Lord spoke about the "unpardonable sin" in response to some people who ascribed his miracles to satanic influence instead of divine. They declared, "He is possessed by Beelzebul,' and 'He casts out the demons by the ruler of the demons'" (Mark 3:22). It is therefore a very serious thing to ridicule the faithful work of a servant of God. Since we live in the light of the gospel, we should be careful to avoid offending God's Spirit with flippant, careless behavior. Wilson Hogue says, "Every resistance of truth and divine influence, every refusal of light, and rejection of His testimony, and every willful transgression, is a step toward the final rejection of the Holy Spirit, which an infinite compassionate God can refuse pardon."

So the nature of the sin against the Holy Spirit does not rest on a single transgression. It does not rest on a deed or committed act of which people fear that they might have committed. What then is the sin against the Holy Spirit?

a. It is our often-repeated answer of no, no, no to the Holy Spirit in His prompting for reconciliation with God.
b. It is our long, continued rejection of the Spirit's testimony to our hearts, convicting us of sin.
c. It is our daring and obstinate rebellion against the Spirit's gracious influence.
d. It is our deliberate and persistent rejection of His repeated calls to penitence.

So when we talk about the sin against the Holy Spirit or the blasphemy against the Holy Spirit, we do not talk of one act or one deed or transgression. We talk about a state of mind and a disposition of the heart in which a person makes an ongoing rejection of the Holy Spirit. This results in a cold heart and a stubborn mind that both ignore and resist the promptings of the Spirit. At other times—though our actions, attitudes, and dispositions have offended, grieved, and quenched the influence of the Holy Spirit—He does not leave us. He continues to strive with us.

It is the ministry of the Holy Spirit to lift up Christ and lead us to Him, to convict us of our sin, and to put the fear of God in us. He then facilitates repentance in our life and leads us in the experience of salvation and reconciliation with God.

One New Testament word for sin (*hamartia*) literally means "the missing of the mark," that is to say, sin is missing God's targeted purpose for our life. But in the words of the evangelist John, sin is also "the transgression of the law." So sin is more than a single act that is malignant in nature; it is the malignant nature that causes the act.

Webster defines blasphemy as "the act of insulting or showing contempt or lack of reverence for God" or "the act of claiming the attributes of deity."[1] In the New Testament context, the word *blasphemia* means "verbal abuse against someone that denotes the very worst type of slander; it is by wounding someone's reputation by evil reports or evil speaking." Blasphemy also can include "resistance against the convicting power of the Holy Spirit".

Jesus says that every sin will be forgiven us, except the sin against the Holy Spirit. He says that every blasphemy against the Son of Man or even against the Father will be forgiven, except the blasphemy against the Holy Spirit.

The sin against the Holy Spirit or the blasphemy against the Holy Spirit is referred to as the "unpardonable sin." Those who have arrived at this point have no concern about the salvation of their soul, and they live a nonchalant life with a total disregard of God, His Word, and the manifestations of His grace. Thus, the Holy Spirit ceases to strive with them, not because of His inability to help them, but because of their inability and unwillingness to respond to Him.

This is the saddest state of any individual—to place oneself beyond the effects of God's grace through constant rebelling against and resisting of the Holy Spirit. For this reason, Scripture sternly warns us to "grieve not the Holy Spirit," "quench not the Spirit," and resist not the "Holy One." It is possible to cross the point of no return.

---

1. *Merriam-Webster Collegiate Dictionary*, 11th ed., s.v. "Blasphemy."

Afterword

In our journey through Scripture, we have encountered truths that have stirred our thinking, warmed our hearts, and possibly raised some questions. I am confident that we may see things differently at some points, and that is quite healthy. But God's stated desire for us, His explicit commandment to us, and the principles of His Word should be quite clear by now.

It is unmistakably clear that God desires holiness for His people: "You shall be holy, for I am holy" (1 Pet 1:16, quoting Lev 11:44). He earnestly desires this because He has predestined us "to become conformed to the image of His Son" (Rom 8:29). Holiness is more than a biblical teaching. It is a transformative experience, a lifestyle into which God invites us in the power of the Holy Spirit. It is a state of being in which the self is abandoned, the will is surrendered, and the heart is broken before God so that Christ is formed in us. It is a practical way of life in which we are enabled to love God completely, love other believers sacrificially, maintain ourselves spotless from the world, and avoid the very appearance of evil.

We do not receive this experience through any merit of our own, although we must embrace the full grace of God and be willing to present our bodies a living sacrifice to God. Such an experience in the power of the Holy Spirit enables us to love God supremely, live in harmony with the brethren despite our differences, and give priority to the advancement of the kingdom of God. Thus, the apostle says, "Pursue peace with all *people*, and holiness, without which no one will see the Lord" (Heb 12:14 NKJV).

If we subscribe to the Bible's teaching on holiness and yield to the Holy Spirit so that we walk in the holy fear of God, the church will truly represent Jesus Christ. Our missional task will come alive. The world will take notice that we have been with Jesus.

CPSIA information can be obtained at www.ICGtesting.com
Printed in the USA
LVOW112004091111

254284LV00001B/2/P

9 781593 175122